Celebrating 50 Years of *Frontier* (1968-2018)

Hope and Transformation

Selections from *Frontier*

Celebrating 50 Years of *Frontier* (1968-2018)

Hope and Transformation

Selections from *Frontier*

Edited by

Timir Basu

Anirban Biswas

AAKAR

Hope and Transformation: Selections from *Frontier*
Edited by Timir Basu and Anirban Biswas

First Published 2018

ISBN 978-93-5002-561-1 (Pb)

Published by
AAKAR BOOKS
28 E Pocket IV, Mayur Vihar Phase I
Delhi 110 091 India
aakarbooks@gmail.com

Laser Typeset at
Arpit Printographers, Delhi 110 032

Printed at
Sapra Brothers, Delhi 110 091

Contents

Editors' Note

The book is a collection of sixteen articles published in the recent past in *Frontier*. The weekly, first published on 14th April 1968 has now completed its fiftieth year, and it is perhaps appropriate that such a collection should be published. We grappled with the idea of preparing such a volume for quite some time, but somehow procrastinated. It is mainly due to the enthusiasm and prodding of K.K.Saxena, founder of the illustrious publishing concern, Aakar Books, that this volume is able to see the light of day. In fact, he has made us conquer our indolence, and has supervised the work of copyediting and printing with meticulous care. To him, our indebtedness is boundless.

Selection of articles for the volume was not an easy affair, particularly in view of the fact that a many excellent and thought-provoking articles have been published in *Frontier* over time. This volume could not be made too large, and we have no illusion that we have been able to include all the articles that deserved to find a place here. We crave the forgiveness of those whose articles we have been forced to leave out due to lack of space.

It may be recalled that in the late 1970s of the last century, a two-volume *Frontier Anthology* under the heading *Naxalbàri and After* was published with Samar Sen, Debabrata Panda and Ashis Lahiri as editors. That *Anthology* received a warm response from those interested in the subject. Time has changed much since then and hence the contents of the present volume have got to be somewhat different.

We are extremely grateful to Professor Anup Sinha, who agreed to go through the entire range of articles and write an introduction to the volume. Thanks are due to all the others who have encouraged us in this endeavour. It is hoped that the outcome of our efforts will be appreciated by the readers.

14 April 2018 **Timir Basu & Anirban Biswas**

Introduction

The name *Frontier* will not be familiar to young people of the current generation, but those who grew up in the 1960s and 70s would have certainly heard of the publication and its founder editor, Samar Sen. Rarely is a periodical's standing so intricately connected with the fame of its editor. After Samar Sen's death some well-wishers of *Frontier* made concerted efforts to keep the memory of Samar Sen alive. The periodical is still published regularly though its readership must have shrunk considerably when compared to what it was forty or fifty years ago. This volume is an act of looking back—a retrospect with a collection of sixteen articles. The articles have been selected from past issues over the last two decades. The oldest article is one published in 1994.

Frontier was known as a left-wing publication, sympathetic to the cause of the Naxalite movement in India. With left-wing politics in retreat in the country and very few young people even interested in such ideas and politics, such a volume could easily be seen as a mere curio from the past, or worse still, a collection without any contextual relevance. The Editor, Timir Basu and the Assistant Editor, Anirban Biswas have put together a seemingly unrelated set of articles which were published in *Frontier* over the years. One might raise a question about the purpose of putting together such a volume.

Two things can be said in its defence. The first reason is that one gets a remarkably good idea of Samar Sen—the man and his times. The pieces by Timir Basu, Anirban Biswas and Partha Chatterjee in their various distinct ways portray the many facets of the persona of Samar Sen—the human being, the journalist, the poet and his commitments. The second purpose is polemical. *Frontier's* image as an anti-establishment journal was well known. It was a space where all those who could not publish in mainstream media were welcome. The articles in the journal were passionately political, fiercely critical, articulated against state violence targeted at people's movements. The critique would carry over to the established left which was open to using the state machinery for political gains.

The selected articles in this volume cover a vast range of issues in left politics. All of them are relevant even today—from the lesson from the past history of revolutionary movements to the rise of neoliberalism and fascism in contemporary India. It is a reminder that the issues which formed the content of debates in the 1970s and 80s are still unresolved, though the social context may have changed. Oppression, lack of democratic rights, devastation of human habitat and the natural environment, the politics of identity and difference—all remain everyday issues in the contemporary world. If anything these issues have become more complex and more inhuman with the passage of time. Hence the volume serves the purpose of pointing out problems that bind us together across time.

There are some pieces that raise voices from the past. The article by Hiren Mukherjee looks back at the left movement in India, its rise and fall, and the role of the Communist Party of India. He looks at the left movement with nostalgia and sadness about things that did not turn out as expected. He ends on an optimistic note that perhaps somewhere in the future young people will be able to change the world for the better. Paresh Chattopadhyay presents a translation of letters written by Romain Rolland to Joseph Stalin during 1935 to 1937. The letters are poignant reminders of the fact that class struggle would intensify in the building of the socialist state and violence could be inevitable. Rolland obviously is aghast at what the Stalinist regime was allegedly doing in suppressing opposition. Dipanjan Ray Chaudhuri in his piece on the 'Party and Commune' discusses the shortcomings of the Paris Commune, the Soviets, and the Shanghai Commune experiences in not doing enough to give the workers adequate empowerment. There were tactical mistakes and somewhat infantile errors, but all the organizations had, albeit in an embryonic form, a degree of workers' control and pluralistic democracy. In a similar vein, Vaskar Nandy presents a critique of the socialist state and the dictatorship of the working class as has been historically observed in practice. He emphasizes the democratic deficit and argues for movements built on greater democratic freedom which gives the working class the ability to make mistakes but also learn from them to become the new ruling class.

There have been debates within the left discourse on revolution as to the constitution of the revolutionary vanguard. The subalterns in the standing army have often been cited as part of the working class with an ability to provide organizational leadership, not only to lead other oppressed people but to sabotage the armies of the ruling powers from within. The article by Peter Custers examines the significance of one such abortive movement in Bangladesh in 1975 led by an army officer Colonel Abu Taher.

Contemporary India has been struggling with issues of the rising hegemony of neoliberal ideology, identity politics, aggressive nationalism in the form of Hindutva, and tribal movements across India. Santosh Rana examines the roots of identity politics and the interrogation of caste hierarchies that emerged as an expression of the oppressed masses. Gradually, in many instances, the movements have been appropriated by the ruling state, leaving a vacuum that has to be filled. Such movements need to negotiate the dialectical tension between social identity and material deprivations. Ranjit Sau in his piece on 'The Tribal Question in India' presents a historical picture of the role of tribes in the making of civilizations. It has been a long history of exploitation through deprivation and division. Yet tribes have been used to contribute to modern economic growth for centuries. Sau, however, points out that in India the movements of tribes against the modern Indian state have been based on violence without an explicit programme. What could be possible when bullets run out, or more likely the last person is dead? Revolutionary movements cannot be based on the agenda of violence alone. Subhas Ghatade has written on

'Neoliberalism, Hindutva and Revolutionary Movement'. He analyses the Narendra Modi government and its objectives where the liberal offensive takes two lines of attack. One, of course, is the soft persuasion through media and mass communication. The other is through more coercive attacks by the Hindutva army of nationalist supremacists. Contemporary India resembles a caricature of Islamophobic patriarchy dressed up as neoliberal modernity.

Religious violence is not restricted to Islamophobia alone. There are many other forms of religious violence too. Aloke Mukherjee has a piece about the killing of Abhijit Roy in Bangladesh by Muslim fanatics. Mukherjee examines the question as to why people fall back upon religion as a source of faith and solace, and also how the state uses religion in its agenda to control and coerce. Without broad-based movements involving the oppressed masses, according to Mukherjee, these acts of terror cannot be controlled, and their real character revealed as an instrument of power of the ruling classes. Gayatri Spivak in her piece 'From the Last Dancer' discusses the complexities and pluralities of postcolonial Africa and the role of violence in the construction of states. Africa has a special significance where the colour 'black' comes in as an important element of identity. Spivak reviews some of the ideas of the major scholars and activists in this context. Jan Myrdal's article is actually a speech he delivered to a meeting of the people of Kashmir and Palestine to offer solidarity in their struggle for peace. In his call to 'Stop the War', Myrdal stresses the importance of solidarity in revolutionary strength. This concrete support is more important than ideological proximity to the cause of the struggling people. T. Vijayendra discusses the significance of non-violence in modern Indian political history, especially with reference to Gandhi. He points to a gap between Gandhi's ideas and what he and his followers actually practised. Pointing out that violence, even if abhorrent, is often inevitable in the moments of great social and political change. Non-violence has often been used to divide people and classify all other movements as oppressive and non-revolutionary in character.

The piece by Saral Sarkar on 'Eco-capitalism – Can it Work?' is an issue about the future of capitalism, where a transition might take place not because of the economic crisis generated by the working of capitalism in the realm of the pure economy, but because capitalism's business-as-usual model devastates the ecology and natural environment of the planet. A question has been raised whether capitalism can reform and amend its institutions so as to create a green and nature-friendly 'eco-capitalism', or whether the new system that will perforce emerge if the planet is to remain inhabitable will be devoid of private property and perhaps better described as 'eco-socialism'. It is not something that is to be considered as a thing of the distant future, but rather a thing that has to be built-in into all people's movements, and questions be constantly raised against the established institutions of power and oppression.

This short write-up is not meant to be a review, but rather an introduction to the volume. However, I will share with the reader my own understanding of the significance of this volume. First, almost all the articles touch upon violence as a means of change or control – could be revolutionary, could be perpetrated by the state. The second issue common to all the articles is some discussion of social change. The unspoken link between the two is power. The pieces are different voices against violence and oppression, about the complexities of struggling for a new world, and about many forms of struggle and above all, the importance of discussing and debating the significance of histories and events. There is not one answer to all these questions. There is not one model of an alternative. However, this volume is presented to all who would wish to actively think about changing the world we live in now, and imagine a better world. That world is unlikely to be perfect, but one where violence and deprivation will be less. To all those who dream that one day all these discussions will become an irrelevant thing of the past.

Anup Sinha
Former Professor
Indian Institute of Management, Kolkata

PART I

Frontier–Struggles and Defiances

1

Frontier and Samar Sen

Timir Basu

I used to read *Frontier* from the very beginning, but did not know where its office was located. Even in the 1970s of the last century, when I began writing for *Frontier*, I had no knowledge of it. I heard that the office of *Frontier* was situated in an old building, 61, Mott Lane, in the lane behind the Jyoti cinema hall. The Bengali weekly *Darpan* was also published from that building. The Jyoti cinema hall no longer exists. The alley Mott Lane has long been renamed Manilal Saha Lane by the Kolkata Municipal Corporation, although *Frontier* has been using "Mott Lane" as its address. Once a Bengali daily called it 'Frontier's lane'. I first went to the office of *Frontier* possibly at the end of 1978 or at the beginning of 1979. But my first appearance in *Frontier* was, however, in 1975. It was a piece on the contract labourers of the Calcutta Electric Supply Corporation. I was then trying to organise contract labourers by using the Contract Labour Act of 1972. The *EPW* published that very piece at about the same time and *CALL*, the central organ of the RSP, reprinted it from the *EPW*.

When I began to visit the office of *Frontier*, I did not wish to be involved in a permanent relationship with the weekly. At that time, there were two office employees, and Bhabani Chaudhury to some extent assisted Samar Babu in proof-reading and preparation of articles and notes. Except preparing editorial-type pieces or reading proofs, he could not help much. He did not have time, because he never distanced himself from active politics.

The infrastructure of *Frontier*'s management was somewhat peculiar in nature. It was a private limited company. In consequence, *Frontier* was always troubled with a host of problems, and resultant complexities. Well, these problems still exist because it remains a private limited company. One principal reason was that there was no particularly efficient office worker capable of delivering the goods. *Frontier* could afford to employ only such people who were able to somehow manage things. Perhaps these problems would not have existed had it not been a private limited company, because with the passage of time company laws and income tax laws were, and still are, undergoing rapid changes.

The result was that it was extremely difficult for a small organisation to survive in the face of legal constraints. There was very little income, but the summons of the income tax department used to pour in regularly. It was a company only in name, because its resources were meagre. Yet various directives used to arrive from the office of the Registrar of Companies. Whether the members of the board were regularly present or not, it was obligatory to show regular board meetings on paper. Samar Babu was always troubled by such problems, since he had to do all sorts of works. At night, while in his residence, he used to write the minutes book. A Keralite named Jose used to look after the office at that time. He was unwilling to go to the bank. Hence, when any bank-related problem arose, Samar Babu himself had to go. Since there was the provision of overdraft, problems occurred more often than not. One day a summons was served by the income tax department. Samar Babu was at a loss, telephoning Kiranmay Raha or someone else. Well, Kiranmay Raha was a former Income Tax Commissioner and a lifelong subscriber No. 1 of *Froniter*. He would refuse to lose the position even when his eyesight was very poor. Incidentally, I was present in the *Frontier* office at that moment. I accompanied him. It was found that the matter was rather unimportant. It seemed to me that the young income tax officer had heard Samar Babu's name but never seen him in person, and hence, he possibly issued a letter in this fashion out of a desire to make his acquaintance. Advertisements were scarce; yet whenever there was a possibility of getting any, it was necessary to contact the potential advertiser. Since there was nobody else, I myself had to go. Many among Samar Babu's close acquaintances held powerful positions in the world of advertising. It is not that Samar Babu did not ask them for advertisements. But the reponse was very poor, and hence Samar Babu stopped disturbing them.

One event must be mentioned in this connection. M.J. Akbar did not belong to any revolutionary camp in the usual sense, and many did not hesitate to call him a reactionary. Yet Akbar was the only person to have helped *Frontier* with advertisements at different points of time. He did it during Samar Babu's lifetime as well as after his death. Government bureaucrats wield enough power. Had they willed, they could have helped *Frontier* with a few advertisements. But they did not and preferred to avoid the issue. Perhaps they felt afraid. The paradox is that many of them used to inquire about Samar Babu's health. The only exception in this respect was Abhijit Ghosh Dastidar, the regular film critic of *Frontier*. While holding the post of the Chief Postmaster General, Abhijit procured, although not regularly, government advertisements for *Frontier*. He often gave advertisements disregarding the wishes of superiors.

In organisational matters, Rabida (Rabi Sen) was most cooperative. He was also a director of the company. One morning, he suddenly rang and asked me to go to his house, without mentioning the reason. As I set foot there, he said, "It seems that Samar Babu could not take any salary from *Frontier* this month. You take this amount of one thousand rupees and deposit it in the bank." At that time, Samar Babu used to receive a monthly salary of Rs. 800 from *Frontier*, and an additional facility was the telephone in his residence of 15C, Swinhoe Street, Calcutta-700025. After Rabida's death, I went to his house frequently, and whenever I looked at that wooden cupboard, from which he had taken the money, it seemed that Rabida had never deserted Samar Babu during his hard times. Yet Rabida's own financial condition was not particularly good then. There were well-wishers those days, and they still exist. Samar Babu often said, "Talks do not deliver the goods." Perhaps he expressed his annoyance in this regard after hearing from many, "Samar Babu, how are you?"

The problem about the office room was there from the very beginning. The room was in the possession of *Darpan*, which allowed *Frontier* to use it in lieu of a small rent. There was however no deed or document in this regard. Since the two weeklies broadly followed the same path, there was mutual confidence and understanding between the two. "We are in the same boat," said once *Darpan's* editor Hiren Basu. So, the afiair proceeded in some fashion. At first there was no problem. *Frontier* was always plagued by financial difficulties, but the condition of *Darpan* was even more pathetic. Hence Hiren Basu, the editor and owner of *Darpan*, had to spend his time in constant anxiety, and in order to procure finance for his weekly, he fell into the clutches of various kinds of self-seekers. They were small investors interested in the "rejuvenation" of *Darpan*. Once such an investor suggested to Hiren Babu that if *Frontier* gave up the room, he would set up a press there, and in that case, the cost of publishing *Darpan* would be drastically reduced. Besides, he argued, *Darpan* would be able to do other printing jobs and remove its financial difficulties. Accepting this advice, Hiren Babu pressurised Samar Babu to leave the premises. At that time, Samar Babu had to work under great mental strain and as a matter of fact, it became very difficult for him to work with normal peace of mind. One day, he told me "I could not find a room after my exit from now. Hiren after all, gave a room and as he is asking me to leave it, I have to do so." Yet no other alternative arrangement was possible, and hence the publication of *Frontier* would have to be stopped. I refused to agree and told Samar Babu, "Please ask Hiren Babu to talk to me." I told Hiren Babu unequivocally that under no circumstances would *Frontier* leave the room. Legally, the tenant of the floor was Prasanta Sarkar, editor of *Basumati*. Sarkar allowed *Darpan* to use it and since *Darpan* did not require so much space, it let *Frontier* have an office there. Samar Babu was reluctant to tell anybody about the problem. But I informed Rabida of the matter and he one day took me to Prasanta Sarkar. Hearing everything, Prasanta Babu summoned Hiren Babu that day and told him clearly not to disturb Samar Babu any more. Even after Samar Babu's death, Hiren Babu once tried to make *Frontier* leave the place. Rabida was then no longer among us, but thanks to the intervention of Nityapriya Ghosh, *Frontier* was saved from ejection. In a word, that tradition continues till date. *Frontier* is without a room of its own. Yet about fifty years have elapsed gradually and 2018 is knocking at our door. In the meantime, the ownership of the house has changed and the sword of ejection is hanging over us afresh. *Frontier* is in peril, a victim of perennial uncertainty owing to various reasons, one of them being the 'room' problem.

The matter of greatest concern is that a new readership is not emerging, or rather new readers are not being formed. In this age of Internet, all, particularly students and youths, are engaged in a type of no-risk politics. There is even no chance that the environment of the 1960s of the twentieth century may be resurrected from spontaneous rebellions witnessed in university campuses. Most of the students are apathetic towards party-based student politics, and are reluctant to give a thought to anything beyond their own ambience. As a result, the appeal of *Frontier*-type journals to them seems to have been very restricted. The fact is that there is an ebb tide in the desire to study. Now the Internet supplies many things and there is the scope of reading books that are not available in print. I once told Samar Babu, "You did not ask me to read *Frontier*, but I read it out of my own urge." Now, it is extremely difficult to persuade anybody to read *Frontier*. The main reason for this qualitative change is definitely political. Perhaps it is a fact that writers are at a loss to understand what they should write in accordance with the demands of time. Many renowned writers have made such remarks. But most of those who talk in this vein are more interested in theoretical issues, reluctant to think about the problems of practice. The leftist movement is unable to raise any slogan that can impinge on the new generation.

Even the election-based parties appear on the scene with slogans whose impact is no longer felt when the polls are over.

Frontier never evinced much interest in publishing organised writing. Samar Babu had objections to that. *Frontier* only reflected the spontaneous elaborations by writers on the national and international situations. Bhabani Babu had disagreements on this matter. But Samar Babu was against the breach of tradition and was in favour of leaving the entire matter to the writers themselves. On this issue, he once told Bhabani Babu, "We never ran *Frontier* in this way." Things are much the same now, but exceptions do occur sometimes. I often try to organise writings based on specific events. I have found that many are willing to write but unable to understand where to begin. In such cases, some initial clue is indeed helpful to the writer. But those from whom 'editorial' or 'comment'-type pieces are commissioned have to be informed beforehand of the subject and the number of words.

There were serious problems about writing 'editorials' or 'comments', particularly during the 1980s. Samar Babu used to encourage almost all writers to write 'editorial comments'. He also asked me to do so when I began to write. Asok Rudra frequently wrote such pieces, as did Gouri Prasad Ghosh and Bhabani Babu. Occasionally Debabrata Panda and Sudeshna Chakrabarty also wrote. Yet the problem of getting contributions regularly and introducing a variety in the subjects persisted. Finally an "editorial team" consisting of Partha Chatterjee, Sushil Khanna, Anjan Ghosh and Rudrangsu Mukherjee could be formed. Swapan Dasgupta and Arindam Ghosh Dastidar of *The Statesman* too wrote, although somewhat irregularly. Partha Chattrejee wrote with a fair degree of regularity. Initially, meetings were held in the office itself, but this arrangement could not be sustained. On most occasions, I had to instruct on the subject through the telephone. Gradually this system too collapsed. Swapan Dasgupta could not write for long owing to the objections raised by his employers. Others too could not continue writing for long because of several complexities in their respective places of work and more than that, owing to enhancement of various work-loads. Partha Chatterjee is the person who contributed most. Subsequently, Oxford University Press brought out a book consisting of his editorial comments in *Frontier*.

Many of those who wrote from abroad are now dead. Among the living, one name that must be mentioned is Jan Myrdal. Withered by years and with a frail body, he tries as best as he can whenever requested to write. Among the old contributors, another who feels concerned about *Frontier* is Gayatridi (Gayatri Chakrabarty Spivak). Ever since Samar Babu's time, she has been helpful with writings and monetary contributions.

I did not have much of an ideological conflict with Samar Babu on matters of principle. On two occasions or so, there were some differences of opinion on publishing some writings, particularly those on China. Samar Babu was some sort of a die-hard pro-Chinese. I have been saying all along that the Chinese are first nationalists and then communists. When their national interests are hurt in the least, their 'proletarian internationalism' vanishes like camphor. Once I had a strongly anti-Chinese piece printed in *Frontier*. Samar Babu then scarcely examined other writings except the editorials. Many readers of *Frontier* were perhaps unhappy at the publication of such a strongly anti-Chinese piece in *Frontier*. They seemed to think that by publishing such pieces, *Frontier* was going against its tradition.

From the beginning, different writings of mine made the CPI(M) a main target of attack. Whether in 'editorial comments' or in 'Calcutta Notebook', most of my pieces had as their theme the CPI(M)'s frantic attempt to maintain the status quo in the working class movement or to set up an aristocracy in the organised trade union movement. Samar Babu had the notion that occasional minor compromises did not do any harm. Regarding many pieces, his suggestion was not to attack the CPI(M) directly and instead use the term 'left' without naming the party. His argument was that the range of attack would thus be somewhat broader and its intensity somewhat less.

Except in such small matters I never had any significant conflict with him regarding the functioning of the paper.

Once some enthusiastic well-wishers became active in order to give *Frontier* a changed shape, rather a new outlook to reflect the changing mood of our times. They thought that the needs of the time required a drastic change in the get-up and that a glistening and polished office room was needed. The main inclination was to enlarge the size and make it colourful. At first, I was also prone to think that perhaps a reorganisation financed by a good dose of investment would enable *Frontier* to conduct its business smoothly. A hawker of north Kolkata once told me that Samar Sen's *Frontier* sold as quickly as a race guidebook. But Samar Babu did not evince much enthusiasm in this reorganisation. He did not try to dissuade anybody, but did not show any interest himself. In passing, he once said, "We do not have the infrastructure to do anything on a large scale. Nor do we have that experience. *Frontier* has survived till today because it is run on a small scale." I later realised how true this statement was. It is entirely true that *Frontier* has been able to suatain itself so long only because of its existence as a small enterprise, although at present even this small-scale existence is becoming precarious. Any attempt to launch a large-scale enterprise would certainly have invited disaster. During Samar Babu's lifetime, once an effort was made to sell some shares and collect some capital. But there were not many shares to sell. The capital that was found after selling was scarcely enough to do any real business. Many well-wishers were, however, against the sale of shares. They had thought that *Frontier* would lose its essential character by such deeds. The matter, however, did not proceed far.

Frontier was born in a period when the political situation, both nationally and internationally, was inflammatory in the true sense. But it began to undergo swift changes at the beginning of the 1970s. In consequence, the number of readers, instead of growing as before, rather decreased. A wrong notion is ingrained in many that *Frontier* is an organ of the Naxalites. The CPI(M) is the principal actor of this campaign. What *Frontier* has always done is to oppose police repression (to put it better, planned state terror) on Naxalites. Since the CPI(M) stood in favour of state repression, it naturally became a target of political attack, and various writings highlighted the failure of their social democratic politics. Some writings on ideological questions in the national and international contexts were published, which had only a very limited appeal to ordinary readers. The long debate on the 'Asiatic Mode of Production' might have influenced only a handful of intellectuals. On one point, *Frontier* remained consistent; its uninterrupted opposition to the Soviet Union. Perhaps that is why a large section of the Naxalites used to read *Frontier*, and read it even now. They are not adherents of any particular party or a specific brand of politics. Their number has also of late declined in a strange fashion. At one time, Samar Babu's life was endangered owing to his opposition to the 'annihilation campaign' of the Naxalites. In an editorial, Samar Babu called them head hunters of Midnapore. This was enough to enrage their leaders. Finally, good sense might have descended on some leaders, and the matter did not move far. The fact is that *Frontier* was harmed to the maximum extent by the ego-centrism and lack of prescience of one Naxalite leader. This leader is none other than Saroj Datta.

The columns written by Saroj Datta in the pages of the weekly *Deshabrati* were then read like hot cakes. In the column 'Patrikar Duniyay' (In the World of Papers), Saroj Datta wrote that the ruling class has three weapons to suppress the peasant struggles—Eastern Frontier Rifles, Frontier Gandhi and *Frontier* weekly. Then he gave the mandate asking nobody inside the ML party to read *Frontier*. It is needless to say that because of this mandate, *Frontier* lost many readers. But many diehard Naxalites did not obey Saroj Babu's mandate. They read *Frontier* on the sly, and even wrote letters to it. It may be mentioned in passing that many of the well-wishers of *Frontier* did not like its staunch anti-Sovietism. One of them was M.S. Prabhakar, the then assistant editor of the *EPW*. Samar Babu published *Kutty*, some portion of Prabhakar's memoirs. While speaking about it, Prabhakar said that he did not believe that the Soviet

Union had gone to the hades. Samar Babu then was, however, not in the office.

There can be no denying that the fall of the Soviet Union and the reversal in China have on the whole generated a frustration among left-minded intellectuals and among the change-seeking people in general. Many of them indeed are no longer interested in studying serious issues. It is only natural that *Frontier* should lose some readers of this kind. Persons not holding any party card but sympathetic to party-led movements are not few in number. Many of them were readers of *Frontier*. Of late, their number has gone down severely, the principal reason being time. Ennui caused by old age has had a dampening impact on them. Yet new readers are not coming, or better expressed, not being formed. The ideology of revolution does not evoke much response from the new generation. One section of those who, during the late 1960s and early 70s, was not afraid to die for the sake of revolution used to read *Frontier* out of their own necessity. That situation is now non-existent; there has been a qualitative change.

Today it is well-nigh impossible to find anybody willing to court martyrdom for the sake of revolution. Writers cannot properly understand the demands of the new generation. There are however turmoils around institutions of higher learning, i.e. the universities. But they are of a transient nature and limited breadth. Participants do not wish to go far because the question of 'career' becomes a formidable obstacle. In the 1970s many among the student community did not give a thought to their careers; they did not care for their bindings. Its impact was felt in every sphere of life, art, literature, films, journalism. Many gave up their studies and research activities and went to the villages in order to get integrated with the common masses, to know and understand the real India. It is another question that their efforts failed, but the boys and girls of those days had the courage to undertake risks and sacrifice middle class comfort.

Yet movements still exist. Institutions like Jadavpur University, Jawharlal Nehru University and Hyderabad Central University have been hitting the headlines. In the context of these movements, many broader issues are also coming to the fore, e.g the *varna system*, nationalism, definition of patriotism, etc. *Frontier* has been, as before, publishing pieces on such movements, giving vent to different opinions for as well as against these movements. Yet it is incapable of reaching the agitators. One possible reason is the over popularity of the electronic media and their ability to reach a much larger audience.

A strange thing is that although all the leftist parties have their respective all-India students' organisations, they hardly launch movements on the common problems of students. And university-based student organisations seemingly maintain some sort of aristocracy. Recently, owing to a directive of the Supreme Court, a complexity has arisen regarding medical and engineering entrance examinations and thousands of students aspiring to appear at the examinations feel helpless. Yet no student organisation is making the minimum noise in this regard. There is no Vietnam war. But there are too many Vietnams in the Middle East. Yet no protest outside the American consulate in any Metropolitan city. It was not really the case in the 1960s. Students were vocal enough to show their international solidarity and brotherhood. American aggression did not go unchallenged.

To the new generation, Samar Sen's familiarity either as a person or as the conscience of revolutionists is getting increasingly thinner. Those who are interested in him are people of yesteryears. Perhaps it is enough that *Frontier* continues to be brought out in the face of many types of obstacles. At least this notion is held by a fair number of well-wishers. Samar Babu once said in passing, "I could not realise that *Frontier* would survive so long." It seems that this is the main reason why he did not stress the improvement of the organisational infrastructure from the beginning. It is indeed an exceptional event that *Frontier* has survived with such a fragile structure.

Many have wanted to know how *Frontier* wishes to observe Samar Sen's birth centenary, whether any ceremony will be held, etc. There are many big and small organisations to hold ceremonies. Most of them are more enthusiastic about Samar Sen the poet. Many of the old people close to Samar Sen are no longer in this world. But many of those who are still alive, in West and East Bengal (Bangladesh), in India and abroad, will reminisce. *Frontier* can only do this much. In short a publication to be titled 'On Samar Sen and By Samar Sen' is all that *Frontier* is hoping to bring out in due course.

[This is a slightly enlarged version of an article published in the Bengali magazine, *Arek Rakam* (June 16-30, 2016), translation by Anirban Biswas]

2

Samar Sen: Poetry and *Frontier*

Anirban Biswas

It is true that even after nearly three decades since his death, Samar Sen, the founder-editor of *Frontier*, is not entirely forgotten, but this gentle colossus is remembered only by a very limited number of people. After his death, he received considerable publicity in the press, but the emphasis was much more on his achievements as a poet and a brilliant student of English language and literature than his standing as a radical journalist, although he had bidden farewell to the world of poetry four decades earlier and in his lifetime scarcely wrote anything on English literature. He remarked in his memoir, *Babu Brittanta*(A Babu's Tale), that one of the reasons for his reputation as a poet was that he was a good student of English. For the last two decades of his life, he lived in penury, editing *Frontier* and ruining himself economically. Between the end of his life as a poet and the start of *Frontier*, there lay a period of twenty-two years. And during those years, there was hardly any remarkable event in his career, except his resignation from the lucrative post of joint editor of the daily *Hindustan Standard* (later revived as *The Telegraph*) in protest against what he considered a cunning device employed by the proprietors to foment communal disturbances. Considering the spinelessness of the general run of journalists in this country, it was definitely an act of exemplary courage and commitment to secular ideals. Taken as a whole, his life and career evoke considerable interest and curiosity. Even when only around twenty, he came to be regarded as one of the foremost modern Bengali poets, who tried to transcend the towering influence of Tagore and were moderately successful. Yet he stopped writing poems when he was only thirty, and subsequently, never showed any sort of nostalgia about his poetry, which had brought him so much fame. He experimented with a number of professions, one after another, in his working life, and *Frontier* represented in some sense the culmination of a protracted process of such experimentation. Before bringing out *Frontier*, he taught at two colleges, worked as a news editor at All India Radio, functioned as a sub-editor of *The Statesman*, served in Moscow as a translator, had a brief stint with an advertising firm, held the post of joint editor at *The Hindustan Standard*, edited the weekly *NOW*, a journal founded by Humayun Kabir. He was fifty-two when, after his exit from *NOW*, *Frontier* was first launched, and he edited it for as long as nineteen years till his death. And this period is much longer than his association with any other institution. Each of those assignments lasted at most a few years—the duration of his first assignment as a teacher at a college in the district of Medinipur of south Bengal was two months only. The association with *The Statesman* was the longest, seven years. It is curious that a person, who could not stick to any of his earlier professions for long, continued to run *Frontier* with an indomitable spirit in the face of tremendous odds. It is well known to the readers of *Frontier* that this weekly was the creation of Samar Sen alone, and while running this paper, he had to struggle constantly against poverty. It may be said that such hardship was alien to him during his pre-*Frontier* days, and to court it at such a ripe age was not easy. Besides, the hostile attitude of the government, coupled with the desertion of many initial well-wishers, worsened the material situation for him. Yet he never sought to dissolve the paper and to seek employment elsewhere. Had he wished, he could easily have got a comfortable and lucrative job, and it is possible that only his name would have been considered sufficient by his would-have-been employers, because he had become a legend in his lifetime. It may be said that his defiance of the lures of money and cheap fame, as well as his commitment to the people rather than to newspaper magnates, was not appreciated by the general run of journalists and their employers, and that is possibly why after his death, his poetry, rather than his committed journalism, received far greater publicity in the newspapers. Highlighting his committed journalism was embarrassing to the journalists serving the *bania* press, and giving publicity to his poetic genius seemed more comfortable.

When *Frontier* was going to be launched, some well-wishers objected to this venture. For example, Nirad C. Chaudhury, who was a sincere well-wisher of Samar Sen and a regular contributor to *NOW*, wrote to him that he, instead of earning his livelihood in peace, was being swayed by temporary excitement, and commented that Sen's new venture would inevitably lead to frustration and mental discomfort. The present writer is inclined to think that subsequent history has proved Nirad C. Chaudhury both right and wrong. Samar Sen had to live in penury, and but for the ungrudging help of some sincere friends, his condition could have been worse. Again, it can be said that had he, like many of the so-called left intelligentsia, succumbed to frustration in the wake of the triumph of counter-revolution in 1971-72, he could not have displayed the Bolshevik spirit—he can be called a non-party Bolshevik—that enabled him to run *Frontier* till his death. Rather the word 'frustration' applies more to those who initially encouraged him in bringing out the new weekly, but later deserted it owing to various ideological and worldly reasons. The reasons were probably more worldly than ideological, because *Frontier* always allowed differences of opinions on contemporary issues to be published in its pages. Although broadly leftist, it did not espouse the cause of a particular political outfit. Sometimes, the 'prophylactic influence' on the deserters was the fear of incurring the displeasure of the ruling powers. Again, some people wrote for *Frontier* in order to receive training in writing journalistic pieces and then to use this training for career advancement. Subsequently, they ordinarily avoided Samar Sen. It may be pointed out that none of those early contributors who stopped writing for *Frontier* ever in their lifetime displayed the courage to court the hardships and risks that Samar Sen had to face while running this weekly. Samar Sen, in his memoir, did not, however, display any malice or anger towards them but wrote that their initial cooperation proved that journalism was not everything about money. A few writers, however, stopped writing when they felt that they had gone bankrupt in ideas and hence were no longer able to write. A famous professor of English literature, an exceptional man among the general run of professors in respect of strength of character, told this writer in the early 1980s of the last century that he was no longer able to think of any topic he could write competently on in *Frontier*. The professor had earlier written many notes, articles and comments for *Frontier*. After the period of his active association with *Frontier* was more or less over, he turned to the cultivation of astronomy and Shakespeare, and wrote some illuminating essays, later collected in a book titled *The Insubstantial Pageant*, on Shakespeare's life-vision, and two books on astronomy.

Bengali students and youths of the 1960s and 70s of the last century knew Samar Sen more as a radical journalist than as a poet, thanks to *Frontier* and partly to *NOW*. Yet all over Bengal, not only readers of modern Bengali poetry, but also students of Bengali-medium schools had a slight familiarity with the name of Samar Sen the poet.

They were taught a course on the history of Bengali literature, and each text book of it had a supplementary chapter, not meant for examination purposes, on modern Bengali poetry, and excerpts of Samar Sen's poems figured in it, along with those of Jibanananda Das, Sudhindranath Datta, Buddhadeb Bose, etc. In the imagination of those dreaming youths who had known Samar Sen as a distinguished poet since their schooldays —although he had given up writing poetry much earlier—the image of the poet and that of the editor of *Frontier* were intertwined. This fact is mentioned in order to emphasize the point that in his youth, Samar Sen created quite a sensation, and acquired a considerable reputation as a poet, although the set of readers of his poetry was discriminating. The poems of

Samar Sen usually quoted in the textbooks belonged to the early phase of his poetic career, i.e. when he was still in his teens or had just crossed twenty. It may be mentioned that two of his early poems were printed in the *Times Literary Supplement* in their English renderings when he was less than twenty. They appeared in an article entitled *Modern Bengali Poetry* by Edward Thomson.

We may reproduce an excerpt from one of Samar Sen's first poems (translation by Edward Thomson):

Where'er you go,
In stillness of some startled moment know!
Your breath will catch, to hear, with sudden dread,
Of Death the muffled, undelaying tread!
Leaving my side, you hope to go—ah, where?
Where'er you fare—
On Leda's shining breast, from Heaven's expanse,
Falls Jupiter's keen glance

From the critical essays on modern Bengali poetry in those days, republished later, it is learned that quite a few poets tried to imitate Samar Sen in content and style. Since the late 1930s till the recent times, literary analysts have written on his poetry, although he, after giving up writing poetry, was not known to have evinced any interest in these analyses and criticisms. About his own poems, he wrote in 1970 in an article under the *nom de plume* Sanjay, "When he (this writer) is forced to look up some of his own stuff, weariness and boredom overtake him."

About his political association, it is worth noting that he dedicated his first book of poems *Kayekti Kabita* (Some Poems) to Muzaffar Ahmed, one of the foremost leaders of the then incipient Indian communist movement. But Samar Sen did not join the communist party. It also needs mention that the contents of these early poems, by themselves brilliant in their form as well as content, betray no explicit influence of communism or the Indian communist movement. One typical illustration is the aforementioned excerpt. From *Babu Brittanta*, we learn that he had close relations with two other communist leaders, Bankim Mukherjee and Radharaman Mitra (a co-accused of Muzaffar

Ahmed in the Meerut Conspiracy Case). There is, however, only one reference to Muzaffar Ahmed in *Babu Brittanta,* informing readers that *Kayekti Kabita* was dedicated to him. It may be noted that Samar Sen's second and third collections of poems were dedicated to Radharaman Mitra (and Buddhadev Bose) and Bankim Mukherjee respectively. In these two collections, and then in the fourth and fifth ones, the influence of the then socialist and communist movement was more clearly manifest. A careful study of the entire range of his poetic creations should make this point obvious to anybody.

By way of illustration, a few lines from a poem, written in May 1942, may be reproduced in their English rendering,

> At this moment of the last gasp of imperialism,
> Stormtroopers of counter-revolution,
> Strive to acquire new empires in countries
> We swear to resist it in this country
> ....
> Innumerable marauders will go into graves
> Capitalism will be crushed all over the world,
> It will disappear in this Hindustan,
> Oh, Government, the Lord,
> The Governor General, the military governor, Alexander, the hero of Burma
> We are yet slaves, but you are captives of your own tricks
> Captives of the grinding machine of history, owing to the self-annihilating fate (translation by this writer)

An excerpt from one of his last poems, written on the occasion of the suppression of the historic naval revolt, may illustrate this point further:

> The day in Bombay left behind the smell of gunpowder; On the streets drops of blood.
> When the staccato sound of rifles
> comes to a stop in the city
> The revolutionary leaders assemble in the field to deliver speeches.
> The railings of the park tremble at
> The shouts of the Sardar
> Perhaps the two hundred and seventy corpses

At the thought of the sins they have committed
The warships, defeated by bluffs, lie
still and motionless at the harbour.
The bayonets, arrogant symbols of the empire, stand on guard here and there
Our freedom is on its way!
The Cabinet Mission is on its way!
Jai Hind

(Translation by this writer)

It is not known what Samar Sen felt when, in 1967, i.e. three decades after the publication of *Kayekti Kabita*, Muzaffar Ahmed denounced the Naxalbari uprising as a CIA-engineered movement. It may be surmised that his respect for the latter did not grow after this sort of slanderous denunciation. When Muzaffar Ahmed died in 1973, Siddhartha Sankar Ray, the then chief minister of West Bengal, payed homage to the deceased. On the other hand, Ray tried every means at his disposal to stop the publication of *Frontier*. In the eyes of Siddhartha Ray then, Samar Sen, the poet-journalist, was a greater enemy than Muzaffar Ahmed, the communist leader. Yet *Frontier* had never hesitated to publish reports on the tragic consequences of the activities of urban Naxalites and thus to risk incurring their wrath. It is again tragic that those who, after coming out of the CPI (M) in the wake of the Naxalbari uprising, formed their own party turned their differences with Samar Sen and *Frontier* into an antagonistic contradiction. They would brook no criticism, even of the mildest nature. This was one manifestation of vain arrogance developing *pari passu* with the all-pervasive left adventurism that came to dominate the movement, the human cost of which turned out to be heavy.

Why was then Samar Sen an unforgivable enemy of the ruling Congress establishment of 1970-77? The reason is probably twofold. First of all, it published reports of state-sponsored extra-legal violence, i.e. cold-blooded murders in the name of 'encounters', and denounced this violence in strong language. Simply speaking, it constantly exposed the falsehood of the ruling establishment. Secondly, it allowed space to the various fugitive or imprisoned Naxalite ideologues for conducting their polemics in the wake of the serious setback received by the movement in 1971-72. Quite naturally, Samar Sen became the *bete noire* of the Indira-Siddhartha combine. As measures of reprisal, the government made lumpen youths owing allegiance to the Congress attack the office of *Frontier*. Government advertisements were stopped, and stall-owners were asked not to sell *Frontier*. Siddhartha Ray's police however did not arrest Samar Sen, probably considering it a somewhat risky business. It was easy to arrest and torture those who may be called ordinary mortals, but not a person of Samar Sen's stature, more so because *Frontier* was published as a legally registered weekly, and it was difficult to implicate its editor in murder cases.

It is true that the Left Front Government too did not show any type of generosity as far as advertisements for the weekly were concerned. The reason was simple; Samar Sen could not become one of their uncritical supporters. He hailed the defeat of Indira Gandhi and his party in the Lok Sabha and assembly polls of 1977, but could not be very optimistic about the Left Front Government. The defeat of and splits among the Naxalites had left a depressing effect on his mind, but he could not believe that the Left Front Government was capable of bringing about a revolutionary change in Bengal. His caustic remarks, made in *Babu Brittanta*, on Jyoti Basu's reluctance to try and punish the tyrannical police officers of the Indira-Siddhartha regime of 1970-77 must have exasperated the ruling left. He commented that fortunately, Jyoti Basu was not on the jury of the Nuremberg trial, because had he been so, the Nazis who had carried out the behest of their master would have been acquitted. It is true that the tyrannical police officers, who were engaged in the cold-blooded killings of unarmed youths during the Indira-Siddhartha regime, got frightened after the dethronement of the Congress in 1977. But the lukewarm, almost apathetic, attitude of the Left Front Government and its chief towards their trial and punishment allayed their fears. This very attitude also disheartened the potential witnesses of the crimes of the police.

Lack of official support robbed most of them of the courage to come out openly to give evidence on such killings.

For an appraisement of Samar Sen's life and work, we may in all fairness quote from a book, *Tari Hate Tir* (From the Boat to the Bank) written in Bengali by Professor Hiren Mukherjee, the famous CPI parliamentarian and orator. " Samar Sen's young talent showed the potentiality of kissing the sky as early as 1937-38. I say this deliberately in order to anger and please him at the same time. But a poet must have intellectual balance, and without calmness of mind, the fertility of creation gets dried up. Perhaps because of this, the man, a repository of virtues, and liked by many of us, quickly withdrew into silence, engaged himself in many useless deeds for many years, acquired fame by writing prose in a foreign language, but Bengali poetry got him no more. So we now find his enthusiasm for social revolution expressed in articles written in unalloyed English. How can this make much of an impact on this country's social milieu?" Professor Mukherjee perhaps meant that Samar Sen should have continued to write poems and added to his reputation as a poet, but he was restless in temperament and hence his creativity dried up. There is nothing to prove or deny this hypothesis. Again, it is true that the impeccable language and style of his editorials written for *NOW* and *Frontier* formed an additional attraction of these two papers. Quite a number of people used to read *Frontier* in order to enjoy the dessert of Samar Sen's English prose. But Samar Sen was not a revolutionary theoretician, nor did he pose himself as one, and he was aware that the role of a weekly, whether published in English or in Bengali, in any radical transformation of the society cannot but be limited. But notwithstanding his choice of a 'foreign language'for giving expression to his social and political concerns, there can be no doubt that *NOW* and *Frontier* served the cause of democracy and freedom in this country in a way that has few, if any, precedents in the world of periodicals. Again, the fact that he continued to run the weekly for so long does not accord well with the image of an intellectual with a restless mind. Somewhat irrelevantly, it may be added that

Professor Mukherjee too acquired fame as a graceful writer of English prose and as an excellent orator in English.

After Samar Sen's death, *Anustup*, a Bengali quarterly, brought out a special issue on him. *En passant*, it may be mentioned that preparations for this issue had started when he was still alive, but when the preparations were in progress, he was overtaken by death. It was published a few months later. In an article appearing there, Partha Chatterjee accurately pointed out that despite its specific political outlook, *NOW* stood in the centre of the cultural world of the educated Bengalis. But owing to the changes in the Bengali mind that had taken place in the 1970s, Samar Sen could no longer remain where he had been, and hence *Frontier* became the voice of only the downtrodden, the tortured and the marginalized. Twenty-seven years have elapsed since Partha Chatterjee wrote this piece. Yet *Frontier* continues to exist, upholding the same principles, giving space to those for whom there is nobody else to speak. In Samar Sen's poetry, there was the blossoming of a socially conscious, sharp personality, and in *Frontier*, the culmination, and the fruition of it. It was a transition, an upliftment. In poetry, we find the first spark of commitment, and in *Frontier*, the transformation of this spark into fire. In poetry, there was the flower of youth, and in *Frontier*, the fruit of maturity. The intervening period may be called a period of gestation, but the roots of the transformation were definitely there, particularly in *NOW* of the later phase. That was a period of excitement, fuelled by the surging leftist wave. Then the Naxalbari uprising took place that ushered in a new era. *NOW* was influenced by this tide and *Frontier* was born when it was growing. Twenty-eight years have passed since Samar Sen's death and yet the regular publication of *Frontier* has not stopped. This is the forty-eighth year of the weekly and it continues to be brought out, thanks to the incredible perseverance of its editor, bearing the name of its founder. (Autumn Number, 2015)

3

Thinking Aloud

Hiren Mukherjee

Frontier's request that I think aloud for a while in its pages is a welcome surprise. In spite of physical and other constraints and with some trepidation I respond, however inadequately.

I recall how in 1964, having written a book on the just deceased Jawharlal Nehru and confessed, in the process, that I knew I had not been "a good enough Marxist", I was hauled over the coals and accused of being a fake communist. This was even said in black and white in a reputed weekly by at least one learned Marxist well up, indeed, in the niceties of the English language.

Since then, I have had the delectation in the early 1980s (before Gorbachev) of being described by the present-day leader of the rather jauntily named 'United Communist Party of India', Mohit Sen (of whom I still am fond) as a senile sectarian. This appeared, if one cares to know, in the well-known ex-'communist' weekly, *Mainstream*.

Entitled now to anecdotage, I remember in a flash that once, in the late 1960s or early 70s, a group in Delhi's Jawaharlal Nehru University (JNU) asked me over for a talk and in a superior, smirky fashion gave me a delicious dressing down as a "revisionist" never using the word but making me remember how in the 1967 elections large areas of Calcutta used to reverberate to the cry of "Sodhanbadi" lisped by processions of children who—bless them!—marched in the processions behind the red flag and without knowing why they wished perdition to my political future.

To my JNU tormentors, I had mustered the courage to quote a piece of Victorian verse: "You call your fathers fools/So wise you grow/Your wiser sons no doubt/Will call you so." Happily, thay all smiled and we had a hell of an ideological session. Samar Sen had not lived in vain.

Much water has flown down the Ganges since then, and I have lived—cursed be that longevity—to see, "on a global scale", the "contrivance" by the Gorbachev gang (with aid from home and abroad) of a counter-revolution in Russia and Eastern Europe with the annihilation of Russia and of what the erstwhile GDR had called "really existing socialism." I have been witness also to virtual acquiescence in this lethal act by a large part of the world socialist movement praising 'perestroika' and unhistorically hymning pure 'democracy' presaged, many fancied, by the unfamiliar but elegant Gorbachev garrulity. I hate to have to say it, but the way in which garbed counter-revolutionary solemnities were swallowed by the wide strata of the left suggested their having been soulfully syringed with what someone once called "the dreary drip of democratic drivel." It is a case of 'small mercies' that India's biggest communist formation, CPI(M), behaved with a certain maturity and offered some ideological resistance. It is a pity that its preoccupation with parliamentary, parochial and other populisms turns its energies more towards spectacular "rallies" rather than preparation for revolution. This is a stern and in Indian conditions, a task which is of course easier to talk about than to get the job starting to be done.

Many of us perhaps have been too beguiled by old Plekhanov's formulation that in our age mankind had only to be seated "in the historical locomotive" that would reach us to the realm of socialism. That the running of the locomotive implied massive, multitudinous, multiform human organisation and activity was perhaps rather glibly forgotten and faith was put in "the processes of history" ineluctably taking us to the non-acquisitive and non-exploitative society. May be we were never so naive and remembered Karl Marx's warning that it would take many years for us to change ourselves before we could change society. But the visible advance of the countries of socialism along with the apparently promising prospect of cordiality and cooperation between socialism and national liberation all over the globe gave rise to an easy optimum about the future that counter-revolution in eastern Europe has given a shattering blow. History, as Engels said, is a cruel goddess and punishes default, the illusion that before too long a sublime Monday morning would herald the success of socialism over much more than the one-third of the globe it seemed to have won lies broken. One cannot tell for how long the expected processes of history have been held back, but one must no longer minimise the dangers and the difficulties of the world predicament. Didn't Mao Ze Dong in one time predict, in his own fun-filled fashion, that the world victory of socialism may take several centuries? Asked about the impact of the French Revolution of 1789, he had once replied that it wasn't time to be sure, for only two hundred years had gone by since. I do not know for certain if Mao endorsed Stalin's thesis (proved luminously correct today) that class struggle intensifies along with the advance of socialism, but I have no doubt that it was basically the same nation as Mao's unforgettable and perennially evocative summons to toiling humanity: "Never forget the class struggle!"

Recently I chanced upon an item in the day's newspaper (June 28, 1994) to the effect that Pakistan allegedly had "got hold of key Indian defence plans." Whatever the truth or motivation of such news, it put me in mind of an early appearance in the First Parliament (May 1952) when we had asked if India's naval code was known to the United States, to which no answer could be given by the government for 'security' reasons. In a flash we asked a supplementary: 'Can the minister assure us if our naval code was known only to ourelves?' Ironically, to this also, no answer was given—for reasons, also of 'security'! Parliamentary pranks can be pretty entertaining but they touch "how small a part of all that human hearts endure."

The thought comes irresistibly that even in these menacing

times the irrelevance of our politics to real life problems seems to be peculiarly and deliberately fostered. It is little good continuing to rue the historical failure of all of us in India, not alone the Congress, to prevent the unholy purchase of our country at the cost of partition, involving for the future the fact of the 'West' to plant a time bomb to be switched at will against India and/or Pakistan. It is also a fact that Pakistan's virtual 'subservience' (more than India's) to the 'West' has added special and noxious complications to the situation. Even as we always try to pose as injured innocents (in so far as India-Pak istan relations are concerned), can it be denied that all of us, including Communists and the Left generally, have badly defaulted in this regard? One wonders why serious national debates (in and out of Parliament) hardly ever takes place on such issues as Pakistan-India relations, or even, relatedly, Kashmir (and Punjab, or the critical goings-on in the north east). The Left is alleged to have a strategically vital position in Parliament, but why does Parliament fail not only over Bofors, the Manomohan 'scam', the Harshad Mehta-Prime Minister tie-up, etc. etc, but even over other possibilities—reported bright on account of today's 'non-confrontationist' political climate—of revivification of decent relations, if not yet friendship, with Pakistan? This sort of talk would seem abracadabra to most people, but at least the Left pause to ponder that, in February 1953, Stalin had given his last interview to our ambassador K.P.S Menon, during which, while deploring the concept of religion as the basis of the state, he had asked Menon if India had ever considered the idea of a confederation that, to Stalin's mind, was the best device for our subcontinent. Perhaps if Gandhi had lived longer or Jawaharlal had found himself free to overcome habitual inhibitions, progress towards the end indicated by Stalin would have taken place. But I have yet to learn if communists and the Left have even today toyed with this confederation concept. Not that it is an easy job, but must we be allergic to basic ways of thinking and acting for our future?

* * * *

I confess that awaiting the end of a long life and my return to the elements I have been, for quite some years, feeling as if, with the world and my own country going downhill, "out of the day and night/a joy has taken flight." It is a tough job to fight, as Gramsci advised long ago, pessimism of the mind by "optimism of the will." I prefer, almost like counting beads, to repeat Rabindranath Tagore's dictum that to lose faith in man is a "sin" that one must never ever commit. I wish, therefore to be able, if I can muster the requisite spirit, "to hope till hope creates/From its own wreck the thing it contemplates." But when I look around, and especially cling, as I must, in my feeble way to the communist movement where I found in my home in 1936 (and in spite of heart breaks cannot breathe anywhere else), I cannot avoid a certain deep-going depression which I would to the devil my younger contemporaries will overcome.

(Autumn Number, 1994)

4

The Reluctant Hero

Partha Chatterjee

At a time when we are being treated daily to the blood-curdling spectacle of a celebrity talk show host threatening to unleash the mobs on other journalists for their 'anti-national' news reports, it seems somewhat futile to even bring up the question of the ethics of journalism. But *Frontier* has always been a journal that stood apart from the so-called mainstream. Its founder, Samar Sen, gave it a foundational strength of character that still, a full century after his birth, allows us to use its columns to remember him as soft-spoken, unheroic, but a resolute defender of the simple virtues of truthful journalism.

Early in his career, Sen was the news editor of a major English daily published from Kolkata. In 1964, following the Hazratbal incident in Kashmir there was communal tension and violence in many parts of India, including West Bengal. At a meeting convened by the Chief Minister Prafulla Sen, the editors of major newspapers and magazines agreed not to publish news or photographs that might inflame communal passions. But a few days later, the Bengali daily belonging to the same media house published sensational reports of the alleged killing of ten thousand Hindu jute-mill workers in Narayanganj in East Pakistan. Sen told the owner of the house that he was unwilling to publish the story in the English daily. Two days later, Sen discovered to his shock that the story had been published in his paper without his knowledge. He was told by his staff that the owner had instructed them to put out the story. Sen immediately resigned. But interestingly, when he later recounted this incident in his memoirs *Babu Brittanta*, Samar Sen confessed that in his resignation letter he had merely expressed his personal dismay and did not cite any principle of journalistic ethics. His friends, it seems, rebuked him for having missed such a golden opportunity of scoring a point against communal politics. Sen also remarks that such self-censorship could be seen by many as a restriction on the freedom of the press, but his view was that in disturbed situations restraint was necessary. In other words, Sen recognised that there did exist a genuine debate about journalistic truth and he had merely chosen his side in that debate. He preferred to see his resignation as a personal decision and not a heroic act for a cause.

This incident tells us a lot about Samar Sen's personality. The decision to give up a secure job in a prominent newspaper house would put him into considerable financial difficulties for the rest of his life. He became editor of *NOW*, a weekly launched by a Congress academic politician who was then a minister in the central government. In Sen's hands, *NOW* emerged as a significant voice of the Left in Bengal. The owner was not pleased. After some exchanges in which Sen was charged with promoting a bunch of "anti-national" writers, he was dismissed in 1967. After this, he never went back to working for a newspaper owner. *Frontier* was born with meagre funds and a pool of goodwill. That was to be his life—austere, dignified, perpetually in need, but always true to his calling.

Under his leadership, *Frontier* became a forum for a range of critical opinion that the establishment—both political and cultural—considered radical, extremist and anti-national. But the journal never signed up for any party or organisation. Instead, it opened up its columns for individuals and organisations which were not welcome elsewhere. These views were often angry, intemperate, dogmatic—sometimes full of slogans rather than argument. Samar Sen created a little democracy wall where these opinions, debarred from mainstream media, could flourish.

But his own journalistic style was very different. His

criticism was sharp but understated. Sarcasm and irony were his chief weapons. In the late 1950s, he spent a few years in Moscow as part of a team engaged in the translation of Indian literature into Russian. Sen was particularly busy with the translation of Tagore's works. While in Moscow, he wrote periodic columns in the *Economic Weekly* of Mumbai and the *Hindusthan Standard* of Kolkata. He wrote about a range of subjects—not only politics and socialist planning but also about daily life in the Soviet Union. He wrote about the de-Stalinisation campaign, Khruschev's speeches, the deification of the cosmonaut Yuri Gagarin, the multiethnic cultural life in the Soviet Union, the reaction to the publication abroad of *Dr. Zhivago*, the Cuban missile crisis, etc. Sen was aware of the fact that he was in the Soviet Union as an employee of a Soviet publishing house. He was also sympathetic to the cause of building socialism. His despatches were never overtly critical. But ever so often, there was just a slight undertone of irony that gave away his scepticism. Take his report on a campaign flagged off by Khruschev encouraging academics, writers and artists to engage in some productive manual labour. That way, the campaign insisted, the quality of intellectual work would also improve. Samar Sen added as comment: " Personally I am for the new scheme. In the Calcutta school I went to, polytechnical training was compulsory and for four years I laboured at carpentry, weaving and dyeing. The result has been most fortunate. I can sharpen my pencil with a blunt knife, thanks to my knowledge and practice of carpentry." The reader was left in little doubt about what Sen thought of the chances of improving the writer's intellectual output by doing manual work. Or again, take the following lines from his report on the the 21st Congress of the CPSU: " Raucous crows cried themselves hoarse over their approaches to the Kremlin and snowsweepers responded with a similar grating noise—this similarity always fascinates me—as delegates to the 21st Congress discussed, applauded and approved the blue-sketch of a communist society. Even an oriental could not take the crows as an evil foreboding: they must be crowing with delight, for prosperity is round the corner; even taxation is to be abolished in the next few years."

Sen was taken aback when one day he was called up by one senior official of the publishing house and shown an entire folder of his reports published in Indian journals along with their Russian translations. He was asked to explain why he had written several untruths about the Soviet Union. Sen explained that everything he had written was based on what he had read in the Russian press and picked up from his conversations with Russians. He was told quite firmly (or so Sen writes) that only what was published in *Pravda* was the truth; he should take nothing else as reliable news. The meeting was very cordial, but the message was conveyed. Sen became very careful in sticking to official versions when reporting on the news. But he did not abandon the note of irony and occasional jabs of sarcasm. After all, he could not be reprimanded for engaging in the writerly art of rhetoric.

For the record, it should be noted that even as editor of *Frontier*, Sen did not shrink back from penning an acerbic comment or two on the tactics of the Naxalites whose cause this journal did more than most to defend. In 1970, when the Naxal Youth brigades targeted the cultural symbols of semi-feudal and semi-colonial nationalism, he wrote in *Frontier*: "But can one be cocksure that the urban tactics seen so far will ever transform the social and political order? That the revolution they talk about will not again be aborted as in 1949? It is not that easy to overthrow a system. Where is the working class in all these activities? However, to the Naxalites all doubters are at best fools and at worst traitors and agents. Let them meditate on the frustrations of 1949—1970 is not 1949. The youths will urinate and defecate on them, not debate with them."

His journalistic ethics were sorely tested during the years of the Emergency. Despite the restrictions on the press and the hassle of getting the text of every article cleared by the censors before its publication, he did not close down *Frontier*. Had he done so, the small staff that worked for the paper would have been left without a job. Instead, in order to publish his weekly on time, Sen chose not to submit any matter, accepting the full risk of any subsequent trouble. Since sales were down, he decided to forego his own salary and instead wrote regular columns in the mainstream press. That is how his memoirs got written. Sen had a very realistic sense of the constraints, both institutional and personal, within which he had to practise his journalism, and instead of railing and ranting against those constraints chose the option which would best allow him meet his obligations as well as follow his professional calling with dignity, self-respect and truthfulness. Some might ask if Samar Sen's personal ethics in the field of journalism were not somewhat elitist, perhaps even snobbish. After all, choosing to work within the given constraints and restricting one's critical armoury to occasional thrusts of critical rhetoric could only work for a rather select readership. In any case, he had deliberately limited that readership by running a low-budget English weekly. In fact, there were occasions when his friends did volunteer to raise the fund for a more glossily produced news magazine of the Left that might reach many more people across India. Sen did not respond with enthusiasm, declaring that he had no experience of working with such publications. Perhaps he suspected he would lose the autonomy he enjoyed as the editor of *Frontier*. In any case, he certainly preferred the small scale.

He also had a good idea of the opportunities offered, rather than the limitations posed, by the divide between English and the Indian languages. In 1962, he wrote, with his tongue characteristically stuck in his cheek: "We do not always seem to remember another great advantage we have over most countries. The Indian Press speaks with two voices—the mother tongue and English. And it seems unlikely that English newspapers will be crowded out by the indigenous press. Our new rich will take to English as they have taken to trousers. The scope for varied news presentation, for speaking with two voices, is thus almost unlimited in India."

Sen was prescient in his observation about the future of English in India. In fact, there are many more Indians now who read English: the number of news outlets in that language, both print and electronic, is growing exponentially. The quantitative change has had many qualitative effects. Apart from content, there has undoubtedly been a flattening and impoverishment of language. The subtleties of argument and rhetoric that educated Indians of Samar Sen's generation strove to master—not just in English but in their mother tongue too (after all, even with the small output from his younger days, Sen still holds his place as a major modern poet in Bengali)—have become a lost art. This is not so much the result of the increasing democratisation of higher education, which cannot but be a good thing, but its effective bifurcation into an elite stream of good English medium private institutions that only the wealthy can afford and a vast morass of of mass education where, irrespective of language, the quality of learning is abysmal. The result is the loss of educated bilingualism of the reader which editors of English newspapers in the 1970s could assume. It is not surprising that journals like *NOW* or *Frontier* cannot be launched today, and even the *Economic and Political Weekly* remains a unique exception. In fact, virtually all news media today, whether elitist or not, runs with the sponsorship either of corporate business houses or state agencies. Samar Sen refused both.

That is why we are perhaps better able today to appreciate Samar Sen's achievements. As someone who never preached, never flaunted his considerable abilities—indeed as someone who was self-deprecating to a fault—he surprises us in these hapless times with his unique courage, fortitude and dignity. He would have scoffed at us, of course, but for our sake we need to remember him as our hero.

(Autumn Number, 2016)

PART II

Then to Now–Defining the Political Horizon

5

Party and Commune

Dipanjan Ray Chaudhuri

The first state the workers tried to build was the Paris Commune of 1871.

The commune made its own laws and carried them out. The members were elected by the people of the different wards of Paris, and it was a permanent session.

* The commune attempted to abolish taxes and meet the expenses of administration by levies on the rich. Houses and buildings were requisitioned for the homeless, care of the poor and the homeless was assured.

* The abandoned factories were to be placed under workers' control, for revival , if possible. Night-work was to be restricted and the collection of fines stopped. Large-scale industry and manufacturing was to be organised through workers' associations at the factory, and one of the aims of industrial policy was the formation of a federation of associates.

* The debts arising from hypothetication of land were cancelled, a measure greatly beneficial to the peasantry. War indemnity, another burden on the peasantry, was not accepted.

* Rents and debts were frozen and only the principal declared returnable over three years (a great benefit for the small businesses and the middle classes).

* The commune declared the standing army to be disbanded, and replaced it with the newly recruited National Guard (mainly workers with an extra allowance) in Paris and a National Militia in the rural departments. The National Guard was to preserve

the arms they carried, choose their own officers and avail of the right to recall if they lost confidence in the officers. The police was converted into paid employees of the commune. No official or member of the commune could be paid a salary higher than workers' emoluments. The right to recall applied to everybody.

* Public education was to be open to all. The Church was delinked from education and other lay matters, and was not to be supported by taxation of the public. Of the 90 members of the commune, 25 were workers, 13 were members of the central committee of the National Guard—15 were members of the International Workingmen's Association (in which Marx was corresponding secretary for Germany, Engels for Belgium).

Apart from the members of this association (in the commune they were mainly Prudhonists, upholders of a 'socialism' of petty production, and opponents of associations of workers in factories and federations of associations), there were Blanquists (highly disciplined, organised secretly almost conspiratorially for direct action against the state). The internationalists and Blanquists made up 25% of the members of the commune the majority of members being under the influence of the idealism of the Jacobins of the French Revolution. Thousands of men and women debated politics and economics day and night in one meeting after another. Municipal elections were held in the midst of the civil war. It was found that all over France there still existed 35,000 communes returning 700,000 councillors of whom only 8,000 belonged to the reactionary coalition of Legitimists, Orleanists and Bonapartists.

Apart from the numerical weakness and unpreparedness of the workers at that point of history and the general untidiness and inconsistency of thought characteristic of petty-bourgeois influence the defeat of the commune was compounded by a lack of correct understanding of the nature of the state and underestimation of the strength of the forces of reaction which had grouped around Thiers at Versailles to act as cat's paw for the Prussian army.

1. When Thiers fled with the army they were not pursued. The commune did not prepare adequately for the return of the

reactionary forces or a seize. Then, and later, the commune failed to smash the regrouping of the bourgeois state at Versailles. This was, of course a difficult task because of the presence of the Prussian army, which declared war on the commune when it seemed that Thiers might not be able to defeat the commune.

2. The Bank of France was not taken over.

3. There was no coordination with the poor peasants. At least three months would have been required to talk to them and network with the communes set up in rural areas and towns (Lyons and Marseilles set up communes which were crushed by Thier's army).

4. While the commune did make political mistakes the alignment and relative strength of class forces were not in favour of revolution at that time. For the commune to win, the old state had to be smashed completely and a new proletarian state set up.

Backed as it was by the victorious Prussian army, Versailles could not be crushed by Paris alone. Before the Paris commune could win over the peasants and consolidate itself as a state in confederation with communes all over France, it was destroyed by the alliance of Prussian junkers, the French bourgeoisie and the French monarchists.

On the positive side, the Paris Commune demonstrated the capability of the workers to organise themselves in locally elected committees with regional committees at different levels formed by delegations right up to the national level, the committees combining legislative and administrative functions, and protected by the armed people organised as a workers' army with democratic internal functioning through elected committees and elected officers, all subject to recall.

The main point was control of the commune-state including the workers' army by the worker masses through the grass roots level elected committee members being subject to recall.

All this had been achieved by a Communist Party, which, however, neither proves the 'This was fortunate' type of comment, nor the 'This is why such serious political mistakes were made' type. But one thing is true. The level, scale and quality of the critical comments handled by the commune could never have been allowed in the communist parties the world has seen, nor would any such party have accepted the degree of control of working masses over the commune. The commune was not only a workers' dictatorship it was a workers' democracy, too, and a pluralistic one to boot.

The next attempt by workers to build a state occurred in Russia in 1917. Once again the workers organised themselves in commune-like structures. Only now they were called Soviets. The first Soviets were called Soviets of Workers' and Soldiers' deputies. Soviets of Peasants' deputies were soon set up but did not have too much influence. At the first Congress of Peasants in May, 537 out of 1115 delegates belonged to the SR. Only 14 were Bolsheviks. The Bolsheviks were a minority in the first all-Russia Congress of Soviets but had a majority in the workers' sections in August. The all-Russia Conference of factory committees of Petrograd elected a central council with a Bolshevik majority. Just before the revolution, the central council had among its 167 delegates 96 Bolsheviks, 24 SRs, 13 Anarchists, 7 Mensheviks. The Petrograd Soviet was the most powerful of the Soviets between February and November 1917, and the power of the Kerensky government depended to some extent on the partial support extended to it by the Petrograd Soviet.

Deputies to the Soviets were locally elected and Soviet power was based on the armed masses. Lenin expected the Soviets to replace the police by the people's militia, the standing army by the armed people, and the bureaucracy by elected officials subject to recall and paid at the rate of workers' wages.

The Soviets were set up by the people. The Bolshevik Party saw and seized on their significance and supported the slogan "All Power to the Soviets." But the Soviets had not been set up by the Bolsheviks, overtly or covertly. In fact, the Bolsheviks were a minority in the Soviets at first, and at one stage when power stagnated in the hands of the revisionists, withdrew the slogan 'All Power to the Soviets'. As their slogan of land and peace caught the attention of the masses, the idea of revolution accepted by the workers and soldiers, and the seriousness with which the Bolsheviks carried out organisational work led to an effective influence on the masses and their activity far beyond their numbers, the balance of power within the Soviets shifted from the Mensheviks and Socialist Revolutionaries to the Bolsheviks. The Soviets held two All-Russia Congress of Soviets between February and November. The political affiliation of the deputies makes interesting reading.

The Second Congress of the Soviets elected finally a central executive committee with 62 Bolsheviks, 29 Left SRs and 19 other socialists. The Right SRs and Mensheviks walked out in protest against the insurrection.

The revolution occurred when the Second Congress was in session. The Bolsheviks had restored the slogan 'All Power to the Soviets'. Bolshevik Red Guards, the workers and soldiers of Petrograd and Kronstadt, and the armed masses occupied building after building till the Winter Palace of the Romanov kings of Russia fell early in the morning. Most of the Mensheviks and SRs had withdrawn from the Soviets, which, composed mostly of Bolsheviks, assumed state power. To carry out the tasks of government, the Congress elected a Council of People's Commissars.

The facts show how the Bolsheviks, the party of revolution won the support of the people in the industrial centres and the garrisons. A temporary alliance with the Left Socialist Revolutionaries extended the support to the villages. The Bolsheviks had well-thought out definite goals, political social and economic, an objective assessment of the situation in Russia, an appropriate programme and a call to rally the people, a disciplined organisation to carry out specific tasks, an experienced, trusted and democratic leadership, cool-headed, yet audacious to prepare meticulously for revolution when that was the task of the day. The Soviets united the people against the enemy, gave then the confidence to fight and chose their leaders. As the Kerensky government dithered, the Soviets had to shoulder some administrative tasks too—a dual state power. The party brought the Soviets behind the banner of revolution, but the actual preparation for revolution and the execution of the insurrection could not be taken up by the Congress of Soviets. It required a party committed to revolution and preparing for it from day one. In Petrograd the Bolsheviks acted through the Military Revolutionary Committee of the Petrograd Soviet.

After the revolution, an increase in inner-party democracy and a significant and increasing role in the administration for the Soviets might have been expected. This did not happen. The central EC of the Congress of Soviets was supposed to promulgate decrees, orders and instructions. The Congress of Soviets was to be the supreme authority and the EC would stand in when the Congress was not in session. In practice, the Council of People's Commissars gave itself the power to make laws and took administrative decisions, sidelining the EC. The EC was supposed to be in continuous session, but actually it elected a Presidium which discharged its functions. In 1921 the EC did not meet more than thrice. The Congress of Soviets was to meet every three months. From 1918 the period became one year. Administration and governance became the tasks of the Council of People's Commissars, and actually the Bolshevik Party called all the shots omnipresent as it was and obeyed by the toiling masses.

Immediately after victory, the party tried to delegate the responsibility of running the factories to the factory committees. But these committees had factory-centric vision regarding what to produce, whom to sell to and at what price. Even the existence of the all-Russia factory committees could not induce a broader vision. For the task of organising nationwide accounting and control Councils of Workers' Control were created under the All-Russia Council of Workers' Control (in which there were only 5 workers from the factory committees and 5 from the EC of the Soviets, the two together outnumbered by trade union representatives). Even then, the coordination of large-scale production into a centralised production by the workers all over the country-wide production and distribution of goods could not be organised and the councils of workers' control were subordinated to the economic councils under the supreme economic council, overseen directly by the council of commissars, these councils consisting of representatives of various people's commissariats and technical experts. Later came the State Planning Commission, the *Gosplan* which partly replaced the supreme economic council.

The lack of organisers with the necessary political vision among the working class led to its relinquishing the power of directing the social organisation of production. Instead experts, even bourgeois experts, enjoying high salaries were brought in and bureaucratisation crept into social organisation of the productive forces. Factories were brought under one-man management enforcing strict discipline to show a profit. An army was set up with privileges for officers including the salute and special forms for addressing 'superiors'. Officers' training schools were set up which inculcated what were practically bourgeois values. A political police was set up known as the *Cheka*. The main characteristics of the Paris Commune were given up.

Lenin noted bourgeois distortions creeping into the Soviets and the party. The Soviets had become institutions for the people not of the people by the people. In fact they had been subordinated to and supplanted by the Ministries of the Council of People's Commissars. The party held real power and they developed a one-way traffic, the party was to lead the people. Lenin was concerned also about the the reverse traffic rectification of the party and was quite agreeable to involve the non-party masses in identifying time-servers ad opportunists within the party but the possibility of ordinary workers actually directing the 'workers' party' ended with his death. Stalin gave a theoretical justification for political domination by the party and practically identified party rule with the dictatorship of the proletariat.

The Shanghai Commune

The 1967 workers' upsurge in Shanghai took the name Commune but actually it was an advanced people's committee of the great proletarian cultural revolution. The cultural revolution was launched almost single-handed to defeat the bureaucratic veterans like Deng Ziao Ping, who were following the capitalist road of Liu Shao Qi. The need to save the party from the Russian type of degeneration into a 'mutual profits club', serving as the political wing of the state bourgeoisie, was there but the movement exploded into a class struggle against bureaucratic bourgeoisie everywhere. Mao had asked for a peaceful movement but he had underestimated the pressure of muffled discontent which had built up, especially the young who had nothing compared to which the present was an improvement. The students and youths responded overwhelmingly to Mao's call of "Bombard the headquarters" and criticised bureaucratic veterans at school, the neighbourhood, and the town and village. There were armed clashes between the forces of vested interests and the Left, and between different factions of the Left. Mao had to bring in the Red Army to preserve peace, although the army bureaucrats were themselves capitalist-roaders, too, as shown after Mao's death when the army generals securitised Deng Ziaoping's ascent to the dragon throne.

Shanghai was the first major town whose workers accepted the GPCR (after an initial blank—not more than 1000 -2000 workers turned out when Chang Chun Chiao, secretary of the Shanghai party committee, first met them regarding the GPCR) and started fighting the bourgeois politicians in power locally.

A million workers gathered together at the city square at one stage. University students met the workers regularly at the docks and the station. Capitalist roaders tried to use a few misled workers to start a movement for material benefits but the movement soon petered out and they had to resign their posts.

The Shanghai Commune was, of course, not really a commune. The Red Army was directed to keep an eye on the protection of Chang Chu Chiao. So, the standing army remained standing by, it was very much there. The power of the Shanghai Commune was derived from the party-dominated state and not the proletarian masses of Shanghai. The importance of the

Shanghai Commune lay in that it had raised the matter of the commune-state, that is the transformation of a party-dominated polity to a proletarian mass-dominated one.

In any case, however, right from the start of the GPCR the pople had taken up arms and in Shanghai, they were used in bitter fights among different factions of the Left. The Red Army was supposed to protect Peking's own Left faction, organised by a young textile worker Wang Hon Wen and allied with other organisations supporting Chang Chun Chiao. Documents with less than 100% provenance but with much internal and mutual consistency suggest that Mao was strongly opposed to the more extreme Left groups who were raising slogans like 'Doubt everything, overthrow everything', (Mao called this anarchist) 'Do away with government heads of section/department' (Mao called it reactionary) in Shanghai and 'Everything about the present-day dictatorship must be changed' (a reactionary slogan according to Mao) in Honan. Mao was worried at the protests against military seizure of the radio station and military occupation of the airfield.

Although the Paris Commune had been referred to in the sixteen articles of the GPCR, Mao was critical of some ideas of the commune.

He thought the commune structure was weak in suppressing counterrevolutionaries and expressed surprise that in Shanghai, the accused were said to walk into the bureau of public security through one door and walked out through another. He pinpointed the vagueness of the form and content of a country-wide structure of communes.

It is clear that Mao was surprised at the volume and ferocity of the people's attack on the party bureaucracy, though he had identified the latter as the headquarters of the bourgeoisie and the target of the class struggle. He did not want the party to disintegrate. He emphasised that 95% of the masses could be won over, after whcih 96% of the cadre would follow the revolutionaries. There appeared no way in which the new, young Left thrown up by the cultural revolution were to pursue and crystallise the new politics of class struggle in the period of the social revolution. The revolutionary students and youths were told to return to their schools and organise in cultural revolution groups at their schools. In general, cultural revolutionary work was sought to be restricted to local limits. It was back to the party, now that the headquarters of the capitalist-roaders had been smashed and the capitalist-roaders were soundly defeated inside the party for the time being. This, as the future showed, was far from an accurate evaluation; they were only waiting for Mao's death.

Mao had raised one important criticism of the commune: its weakness in suppressing the enemy. Indeed, Lenin ignored his own writings on the lessons from the commune in initiating the building of a Red Army (Trotsky was given charge of this) (This was the army which repulsed Hitler). Mao never wavered in his view that without a people's army, the people have no power politically. The commune was clearly against standing armies and for an armed people. It is also to be noted that neither in Russia nor in China was there any general arming of the people.

It is interesting to see, how to save the idea of the party, while countering the Shanghai workers on the question of the commune and the party. Mao, the arch-revolutionary and anti-revisionist, questions the commune, considered to be one of the basic pillars of Marx's ideas:

"If everything were changed into commune, then what about the party? Where would we place the party? Among the commune committee members are both party members and non-party members. Where would we place the party committee? There must be a party somehow! There must be a nucleus no matter what we call it. Be it called the communist party or social democratic party, or Kuomintang or I-kuan-tao, it must have a party. The commune must have a party but can the commune replace the party?"

These are questions which the Chinese workers could not solve before Mao died and the bourgeoisie led by the capitalist-roaders inside the party defeated them and went on to change the colour of the Chinese state. These are questions which are found in the basic dialectics of the workers and their party and as such are important from day one, and should not be ignored as being relevant on a future date after the revolution. The very nature of the revolution and its outcome and durability depend on the answers the workers find to these questions.

(Autumn Number, 2011)

6

Eco-Capitalism—Can It Work?

Saral Sarkar

Since 2007, the world is suffering from an unending crisis. It is no longer only an economic crisis like many in the past; it is a systematic crisis, a crisis of capitalism. Parallel to the futile efforts of the politicians to overcome it, many, even non-communists, are asking whether the crisis can at all be overcome in the framework of capitalism. In Portugal, one even hears people saying the country needs a revolution like that of 1974, which not only overthrew the dictatorship but also tried to build a socialist society.

Against this background in addition to that of the climate crisis, resource crisis and the general ecological crisis one is asking if there is an alternative to capitalism. Recently many people have rediscovered the limits to growth. They have realised that the long age of economic growth and rising prosperity is over. They are now propagating the vision of a "solidarity society" with a "post-growth" economy. Of course, there are now leftists whose alternative to capitalism is still socialism, but one that also cares about the environment.

In this discourse, however, answers to several questions remain relatively vague. What is here "solidarity"? Should a post-growth economy only cease to grow further, or should it contract? Should/can a socialism that cares about the environment be based on an industrial economy?

Also in the ecology movement, there is no clear conception of the alternative. Initially, most activists were radical. Then they soon made many compromises with the existing system. They told the ruling elite that they could create many jobs with environmental protection. In the mid-198os, their mottos were "restructuring the industrial society", "sustainable development" and "sustainable growth." Nobody except the socialists and communists criticized capitalism *per se*. All thought capitalism could be ecologically reformed. Their favourite motto was "eco-social" market economy. Today one speaks of "eco-capitalism" or "green capitalism."

Antonio Gramsci wrote in the 1930s "crisis consists in the circumstance that the old is dying and the new is not emerging." (Quoted in Holz and Mayer 2012: 2)

True, the old, today's capitalism is dying. But is eco-capitalism the new? The idea is not entirely new. As shown above, in Germany, the idea existed since the 1980s. In the English-speaking world, Henman Daly had already in 1977 published his book *Steady State Economics*, in which he maintained that a steady-state economy can be realised within the framework of capitalism. Later, also the terms "eco-capitalism" and "natural capitalism" were used.

In those days, the purpose of the protagonists of this idea was to protect the environment by means of revolutionary technologies. One asserted that it was possible to cut the connection between growth and resource consumption, i.e. to produce more goods and services with less resources. It was hoped that resource-productivity could be increased by factor four or even by factor ten so that despite continuous growth, damage to the environment would go down. However, the existing way of production and consumption would then have to be changed slightly.

But in the meantime, the capitalist system too is in danger of breaking down. Politicians and the bosses of the economy must now save both environment and capitalism. To this end, they have brought forward new ideas and partly realised them. For example, they are massively subsidising so-called renewable energies. In Europe, tradeable emission certificates, the purpose of which is to reduce the emission of carbon dioxide, have been introduced. They are trying to redeem and regulate the finance industry. In short, they say capitalism can be both ecological and social. One is again speaking of "green capitalism". For example, Ralph Fucks of the Green Party of Germany has recently published a book, in which he declares eco-capitalism to be the future of the world. He is demanding a programme for green growth on the basis of renewable energies.

Paradigm Shift

But eco-capitalism, can it work?Well, this writer doesn't think it can.

What is the task an eco-capitalist government must fulfil in order to deserve this name? In short, it must lead the economy to sustainability. A sustainable economy is logically one which is based mainly if not exclusively, on renewable resources. For non-renewable resources would be exhausted sooner or later, and they cause environmental degradation.

Of course they will never be completely exhausted for even ordinary rock contains many useful materials. But an industrial economy needs only such natural resources which contain the necessary raw materials (e.g. copper in copper ore) in *sufficient degree of concentration and* which can be extracted at reasonable costs. In course of time, one after the other, it would not pay any more to exploit particular deposits. (That is already the case with hard coal deposits in Germany). The cause may be a difficult geographical or geological location. Or the degree of concentration of the useful raw material in the one may be too low. That means, the useful non-renewable resources are becoming even scarcer. The renewable raw materials (e.g. wood water) are of course renewable, but also their availability is limited. When the trees in a forest have been felled, one has to wait for years or even decades before the next generation of trees can be felled. And the yearly amount of precipitation is limited by the climate.

In truth continuous growth of the world economy is not possible. When the maximum exploitability of a natural resource has been reached (e.g. peak oil), a zero-sum game begins. Then one economy can get more of a resource only at the expense of others.

This conclusion has enormous significance for economic theory and policy. Directly or indirectly, it has unpleasant consequences for all areas of human life. It necessitates a complete paradigm shift, namely a shift from the hitherto prevailing growth paradigm to what one may call the limits-to-growth paradigm. What appears possible in the former, namely unlimited growth of GDP and prosperity appears in the latter to be impossible. If one accepts this compelling paradigm shift then one must throw much of received economic theory overboard. Then one must also undertake a radical shift in economic and social policy.

If one accepts the said paradigm shift, then one ought to pursue an economic policy that initiates a gradual contraction of the world economy which will only end when a steady state has been reached. After all everybody wants to prevent that today's growth madness ends in a chaotic ecological economic and social breakdown. But capitalists cannot accept such an economic policy, because a growth compulsion is inherent in capitalism. That is why they maintain that sustainable growth is possible and hence also eco-capitalism.

As stated above, protagonists of eco-capitalism place their hope on renewable energies especially on so-called renewable energies. They believe that by 2050 the whole energy need of Germany, in principle of the whole world—can be met through renewable energies.

Actually they already expressed such hopes twenty years ago. Franz Alt wrote: "Just solar radiation contains about 10,000 times as much energy as present-day world energy consumption; the winds 35 times as much; the growth of biomass ten times as much; and hydro-power half as much....Reed grass that can be grown on the fields that today lie fallow in Germany can produce as much energy as all the 21 nuclear power plants of the country....The working group 'Solar Energy for Environment and Development ' of the United Nations ascertained ..in 1991 ...'the total potential of renewable energies is about 10,000 times the current energy consumption of humanity.' " (Alt 1993: 6-8)

Alt also asserted that from biomass people could get raw materials for almost everything: houses cars, every kind of chemical, etc. And such materials could be composted (ibid). And Hermann Scheer wrote in 1999:

"For an inconceivably long time the sun will donate its energy.....And it will do that so lavishly that is could satisfy even the most sumptuous energy needs of the world's humans, animals and plants experiencing drastic growth." (Scheer 1999: 66)

If such visions were realistic then, of course, sustainable growth would be possible, and then also eco-capitalism. Thomas Steinfeld wrote in 2008:

"If one believes Schumpeter, capitalism does not need particular resources. It only needs resources. It perhaps does not even need oil. It might instead be willing without any problem to switch over to alternative energies using the money made on the basis of oil—if the profit is satisfactory. In this total indifference that capitalism shows in regard to the material the economy uses lies considerable hope." (Steinfeld 2008)

Technological Illusions

But such visions are illusions. In connection with the hope placed on solar energy, Barry Commoner wrote in 1976:

"Like sunlight, the energy of falling rain is widely diffused.... and its gentle force would seem to hold no promise of delivering power sufficient to run the energy-hungry tasks of modern society...What transforms the diffuse 'impractical' energy of the rain into the eminently useful power of the hydroelectric plant is the process of concentration." (Commoner 1976: 132)

Astonishingly, Commoner, a renowned natural scientist, failed to notice a difference between subshine and rainfall. When raindrops, guided by *natural topography,* automatically get collected behind a dam, sunshine must be collected by us. Of course, both building dams and manufacturing photovoltic modules involve expenditure of energy and materials. But in the latter case relative to the energy harvest it is much higher than in the former. That is why solar electricity is much dearer than hydro-electricity. In 1976, Commoner had actually hoped that solar energy "can also reverse the trend towards escalating energy costs." (ibid: 122)

Moreover, the low intensity of sunshine on the earth's surface is a cosmological constant. Nobody can change it. People also cannot do anything about the sun not shining at night. The wind too does not blow always. In contrast, the energy content of fossil fuels is very much higher and it is available day and night.

Because of these factors it is highly unrealistic to hope that solar energy will one day be able to compete with conventional energies. Yet, because of their potential dangers, people should desist from using nuclear power and oppose construction of new coal-fired plants. Environmentalists therefore demand that renewable energies be subsidised till they become competitive.

The real problem with renewable energies is however much more serious. If competitiveness were the only problem the state could, by means of discriminatory taxation make the non-renewable energies costlier to the point at which renewables are competitive. But that would not help. For the production of everything that is necessary for producing and commissioning solar modules, wind turbines, etc. From A to Z are are done till today, for the most part by using non-renewable energies. If the latter are made costlier, then also the renewable energies would become costlier.

The real problem with renewable energy technologies is their low to negative energy balance—also called net energy, harvest factor and EROEI (energy received on energy invested). The construction of a power plant including production of all the components that belong to it requires input of energy and materials. The power plant must produce in its lifespan more energy than the total energy invested in its construction from A to Z. That is, its energy balance must be positive. Otherwise the undertaking does not make any sense. There is a controversy about whether solar power plants show a positive energy balance (EROEI). Many, including this writer, doubt that. Such controversy exists also about some other renewable energies. There is a half-consensus on wind-power. Its EROEI is slightly positive according to Odum.

Due to progressively worsening geographical and geological conditions, the energetic (hence also financial) extraction costs of most raw materials—coal, oil, gas, uranium, industrial metals, rare earths, etc—are continuously rising. It is exactly with such raw materials that solar and wind power plants are built. That means, the energy input required for building such power plants is continuously rising. But the average energy content of sunshine and wind remains unchanged. Such being the facts, the EROEI of renewable energy technologies cannot rise. It will fall, in spite of possible technological developments. Miracles will not happen although small improvements are possible.

If the EROEI of renewable energy technologies were really 40 to 70, as claimed by their protagonists, then they would have long ago pushed all the conventional technologies out of the market. For, according to Odum, the EROEI of Middle-East oil is only 8.4 that of coal from Wyoming only 10.5, and that of onshore natural gas only 19.3 (cf. Heinberg 2003: 153). But they are still demanding subsidies. How can one understand that at all? And why does the German photovoltaic industry panic when the government cuts the subsidies slightly? And why did recently—in spite of all the subsidies, several solar technology companies in Germany and the USA go bankrupt? These facts indicate that as Nicholas Georgescu-Roigen (1978) expressed it they are, of course, feasible, but not viable. That is the net energy gain, if it is not negative, is too little for the energy needed to build the replacements (of the same sort) when the life span of the power plant in question expires. Then it is no use saying that such power plants do not emit any carbon dioxide while in operation.

In the final analysis, the subsidies come from the whole (world) economy, which, as all know, is driven for the most part by the conventional energies. How can the renewables replace the conventional energies when they are dependent on the latter? They are parasites. They will die when their host dies.

Another question that must be raised here is why India, rich in sunshine and winds, is still building new nuclear and coal-fired plants. If solar and wind power plants were profitable, i.e. without subsidies, then Indians could easily build a few thousands of them every year. And why do the Chinese prefer to export their photovoltaic modules instead of using them in China for making the construction of new coal-fired plants unnecessary? And why do they have to subsidise their solar module export—the EU commission has ascertained that—although Chinese wages are much lower than, say, Germany?

Of course these are only indications and indirect arguments, no proofs. But they must be considered because the EROEI figures of researchers are unreliable and contradictory (cf. Sarkar). The dispute will be settled in the next ten years through facts on the ground. "In the meantime, also renewable energy enthusiasts concede", writes a Green Party intellectual, "that one cannot reckon with permanently profitable solar electricity production north of the Mediterranean Sea" (Wiesenthal 2013: 29).

For one thing an industrial economy also needs metals and other minerals which are in the main non-renewable and hence exhaustible. For reasons stated above also their energetic and financial extraction costs are rising. Their extraction and smelting also cause serious environmental damage. How do eco-capitalists propose to solve this problem?

They do not take Alt's claim seriously that the society could get almost all needed materials from biomass. They rather place their hope on raising resource-productivity(-efficiency) and recycling. As regards resource-productivity, there are, since long, conceptions that claim that technological development makes it possible to reduce resource consumption by factor 4 or factor 10 without curtailing, even while raising, the standard of living. (See Schmidt-Bleek 1993 and Weizsacker et al. 1995). These are anything but illusions. As Fred Luks (1997) showed, if in the next fifty years resource consumption in the industrial societies is to be reduced by factor 10 and if simultaneously the economy is to grow yearly by 2% then resource productivity must rise by factor 27. This is not realistic. There are simply also limits to technological development of this kind. Most great technological achievements require enormous expenditure of resources.

Also as to recycling there exist totally unrealistic hopes. Thus in the 1970s, Andre Gorz (1983: 83) hoped that "entire amounts of raw materials could be recycled or reused." Environmentalists often say the most absurd idea in this regard came from Professor Jero Kendo, at that time President of the Japanese Science Council. He said we should capture both the surplus CO in air and CO_2 gushing out of chimneys by using solar energy and converting them into useful chemicals in order thus to solve the global warming problem. (cf. Schmidt-Bleek 1993: 80)

But there are also limits to recycling.

Energy cannot be recycled at all. Materials can be and are being recycled, but not unlimitedly. The problem is a law of nature, namely the entropy law. Take, for example, a piece of steel that has been used to make 100 products which have gone to 100 consumers living in different places. After being used up, they land in different landfills. Even if waste separation is practised there, collecting the small pieces of steel and transporting them to a steelworks cost a lot of energy, material and labour. If a part of the original piece of steel has rusted or has been converted into small particles, then it is practically impossible to recycle it.

The above exposition shows that sustainable growth is not possible at all. Also Daly's steady-state industrial economy is simply not possible. For any industrial economy needs large amounts of non-renewable resources which would sooner or later be exhausted or become unaffordable. In the foreseeable future therefore the world economy will inevitably contract. The current world economic crisis is a precursor thereof (See Sarkar 2010 and Sarkar 2012). But an ecological steady-state economy is, in principle, possible at a much lower level than today, for it would mainly be based on genuinely renewable resources of which biomass would be the most important.

But is the transition to such an economy possible within the framework of capitalism? Daly and most eco-thinkers believe it is. There are many reasons to doubt it.

(1) Of course capitalism has until recently been able to overcome many rises of every sort. But that was possible because, every time, capitalists could realistically hope indeed they were sure that the crisis would end and normalcy would come back. Today, however, the prospects are totally different: a long period of economic contraction with the certainty of a stagnating economy at a very low level at the end.

Capitalists need hope and a felt relative certainty in order to be willing to invest. When the objective situation is as described above, especially if the states, out of consideration for the future generations and the environment, pursue a general policy of economic contraction then there is little hope of profit. If the contraction proceeds chaotically with many firms going bankrupt, then there is no relative certainty.

(2) A growth compulsion is inherent in capitalism. In an environment of competition, the motto is expand or perish. Since no firm wants to perish, since all firms must expand if they want to continue to exist, a general growth compulsion arises, also for the economy as a whole. For only in a growing economy can all firms hope to make a profit. And they also thirst for growth.

(3) A big problem is the short time horizon of firms.

Sustainability requires showing consideration for the interests of future generations. But, as one manager said, "a company cannot work for the next generation .....We must now produce for the market and make money (*Der Spiegel*, 9.6.1986 100f)" That is logical. The time horizon cannot...go beyond the amortisation time of capital goods. For profitability calculation... is exactly limited to this time." (Alvater 1986: 100)

(4) Sustainability also entails care for other peoples and other species of nature. This presupposes a moral stance, which is not a part of the principles of capitalism. Since the days of Adam

Smith, the logic of the system says, one should only care for one's own interests. That is still the rule. That is why capitalists cannot care about the social costs of their business. They must reduce their own costs and externalise the social costs as much as possible. The invisible hand, says Smith, will take care of the welfare of society. Smith did not know anything about the limits to growth. But people know today that the welfare of society is to a very large extent the task of the state, and it will be more so in future. (5) If the economy contracts, then also the real income of the people will fall. With the intended or unintended closure of many enterprises, many jobs will be lost. Without an egalitarian distribution of the remaining socially necessary or useful jobs and of the sacrifices that will accompany the process, chaos and social unrest will break out. The world has witnessed in the recent past several bread riots, water riots etc. ... But egalitarian distribution is incompatible with capitalism. That must be a task of the state. Only the state can decide which enterprises must be closed. (6) In a sustainable economy also during the transition to it, there must not be any waste of resources. But that cannot be avoided in capitalism. An individual firm can possibly do that but not the whole economy. Every overproduction, every production of unsaleable goods, every destruction of still usable goods, half empty trains, etc. are waste of resources. The entire advertisement industry is a huge waste. All that must be accepted in capitalism because planning the whole economy is out of the question. Worst of all is the waste of the labour power of unemployed people. But a reserve army of the unemployed is very useful for capitalists. They almost need it. Also strikes are a waste of labour power. But trade unions need it for countering the power of capital. The mass unemployment that pople witness today in South Europe is also making the societies there unsustainable. All that calls for an orderly retreat, a consciously planned contraction, not a chaotic one.

(7) Since economic contraction will (have to) take place on a world scale, world trade will also (have to contract). In order to prevent chaos and breakdowns there must be international

planning and cooperation in this area too. For all this reasons this writer thinks a good society of the future, one with a sustainable economy must be a socialist society. But this time an eco-socialist one.

REFERENCES

Alt Franz (1993) *Heilung flir den blauen Planteen* in Wegwester 4/11993.

Altvater, Elmar (1986) *Alte Hilte mit Gruner leder* in Kallschuer (ed.) 1986.

Commoner, Barry (1076) *The Poverty of Power*, New York.

Daly, Herman E. (1977) *Steady-State Economics,* San Fransisco.

Flicks, Ralf (2013) *Intelligent Watchsen*, Minchen.

Geprgescu Roegen, Nicholas (1978) 'Technology Assessment: The Case of the Use of Solar Energy' in *Atlantic Economic Journal,* December.

Gorz Andre (1983) *Ecology as Politics,* London.

Heinberg, Richard (2003) *The Party is Over.*

Forest Row Holz, Hans Heinz and Leo Mayer (2012) *Krise Hegemonic and Transformation bei Antonio Gramschi,* Munich Kallscheuer Otto (ed) (1986), *Di Gr ilnen—letzte Wahl?*, Berlin.

Luks, Fred (1997) *'Der Himmel ist nicht die Grenze'* in *Frank furter Rundschau* 21 January, Sarkar Saral (1999), London, *The Crisis of Capitalism* (2012) Berkeley Bruno Kem (2008) *Eco-Socialism or Barbarism,* Cologne and Hyderabad.

Idem (2010) *Understanding the Present Day World Economic Crisis.*

Scheer, Hermann (1999) *Solare Welwirtscha fi*, Michen.

Schmidl-Bleek, Frederich (1993) Wievel Unwelt bronchi der Mensch? Berlin, Steibfeld, Thomas (2008) *'Die Krise ols Normalitat'* in *Siiddeulsche Zeitung* Minchen, 18 November.

Weizsacker, Ernst Ulrich Von et al. (1997) *Factor Four*, London, Wiesenthal, Helmut (2013) "DD Solarstrom Lackmustest grliner" Energiepolitik, in *Boll Thema-Es grant*, Berlin. Nr 1.

(Autumn Number, 2013)

7

Walking on Two Legs? Neoliberalism, Hindutva and Revolutionary Movement

Subhas Ghatade

Politics, as the Italian Marxist Antonio Gramsci argued, is always underpinned by hybrid philosophies. Perhaps the best example in recent memory which bears testimony to this seems to be the present dispensation at the centre which on the one hand still sticks to the exclusivist/majoritarian world view Hindutva Supremacism and is simultaneously busy furthering the neoliberal agenda under the glib talk of development.

It is abundantly clear that it hits no qualms in projecting its relationship with a self-proclaimed cultural organisation called RSS—which openly abhors the pluralistic tradition of this part of South Asia, which has been an admirer of the policies and persons of Hitler and Mussolini, which had kept himself aloof from the independence struggle, had opposed the making of the constitution under Dr. Ambedkar and had instead proposed that *Manusmriti* be made into independent India's constitution in a corporate-friendly agenda which is characterised by deregulation of economy, liberalisation of trade and industry, privatisation of state-owned enterprises marked by massive tax cuts for the corporates, reduction of social services and other welfare programmes, downsizing of government, anti-unionisation drive to 'boost productivity', removal of controls on global financial and trade flows.

The grand metamorphosis of Mr. Narendra Modi from a

'polariser' to a 'development man' seems to symbolise this new juncture in Indian politics. He leads a parliament which has the lowest representation of minorities since independence and a ruling party which does not have a single elected member from the biggest minority community in the country. Indians have been witness to a paradox that many members of the ruling party have been found to be valorising Nathuram Godse, the assassin of M.K. Gandhi and spewing venom against the minorities on the floor of the august house.

Everyone knows it but not everyone would like to remember these days that Mr. Modi who has completed around one and half years being Prime Minister of this country remained under scanner of national and international human rights organisations for his alleged complicity/connivance/inaction (during the infamous riots, variously described as carnage/genocide) when he was Chief Minister of Gujarat and was shunned by the leading Western countries for similar reasons for more than a decade. And a case is still pending before the Supreme Court of the country filed by Mrs. Zakia Jaffery, widow of the ex-Congress MP Ahsan Jaffery who was killed by a rampaging mob of Hindutva fanatics in 1992, which similarly calls into question his alleged role during the riots.

In fact, whatever might be the claims of the PR agencies or the spin doctors close to the government—who are busy telling the outside world how Modi has helped raise India's prestige at the international level (forget the fact that the government's attempts to play big brother in neighbouring Nepal have alienated all the mainstream parties from it)—it is for everyone to see that the effects of his ascent at the social level has been devastating.

The mob lynching of a poor Muslim because of a rumour that he was eating beef, in a village not very far from the national capital, and the manner in which the whole barbaric event is being rationalised by different sections of the ruling party and the continued silence maintained by the Prime Minister for a long time, who is supposed to be an avid social media user, is the latest sign of this state of affairs.

What was surprising was that he had come to tweet a condolence message when the son of a famous singer died abroad, but he perhaps did not feel the need to show similar concern when poor Akhlaq was lynched by the mob.

Any stocktaking of the unfolding situation brings home a few stark facts, that with his ascent

- The alleged fringe elements of the rightwing which effectively are part of a continuum have got a new boost/legitimacy.
- With two writers/activists killed within a span of nine months and several others receiving threats and intimidations and supposedly a 'hit list' in circulation, India has of late started imitating one of its Islamist neighbours where bloggers are being hounded and killed and cultural programmes are being bombed supposedly to protect the sanctity of religion.
- Today attempts to foment communal tensions in newer areas are on leading to what the government itself has admitted; there has been twenty per cent increase in communal incidents.
- Retrograde changes in curriculum have been undertaken with people with dubious academic credentials being given responsibilities in key institutions.
- There has been a conscious attack on provisions meant for the marginalised and vulnerable sections of the society in very many ways and there is conscious withdrawal of the state from social welfare activities,
- Every effort is being made to put profit at the centre instead of people's welfare and a free play is being given to the market forces.
- One can see it as a regime which essentially is walking on two legs.

The growing neoliberal offensive couched in the language of 'development' accompanied by (as and when necessary) communal tensions supposedly to drive a wedge between different sections of the toiling masses so that the broader issues of deprivation and pauperisation do not get raised at any level, is the new normal.

As one can see, this tactic has served them well till date.

Despite the growing realisation that they have befooled people by false promises—remember the much discussed promise that they will bring back black money—despite their U-turns on many key issues, despite the fact that prices of essential commodities have skyrocketed in recent times, one does not see much anger coming out on the streets because people can see that the politics of 'us' versus' they' is in full swing. People seemed to be more worried about what is in the neighbour's plate and what s/he is wearing and not concerned with the fact that her/his own plate is rather empty.

Around a year ago, well known documentary film-maker Anand Patwardhan, in his speech 'We and Our Nationhood Redefined'—which was a memorial lecture at the editors' guild—had thrown light on Modi's 'development model' and shown glimpses of what was in store for the Indian people.

Perhaps it would be opportune to quote his observations then about the unfolding nature of these developments:

> "[H]anding over common resources by interlinking of rivers, mining projects and disinvestment corroborated by the stock market is not enough. The ideology must sink roots. The Gujarat Standard Village Social Science Textbook of 2013 in its 8th chapter of 'Our Economy' is evidence of the pervasive ideas of Liberalisation, Privatisation and Globalisation as a panacea for all the problems India faces today.

Consumer rights are showcased, a few individual cases of poor girls and boys making it to an IIT of a just system while on the other hand mechanisms nd policies pertaining to food distribution, education and health care are deliberately downgraded and withdrawn. The idea that the Welfare State has failed its citizens is sold through the mechanism of Public-Private Partnership, to pave the way for the takeover of public assets by private interests. In this scenario a rag-to-riches story is the icing on a cake that few will actually taste. Modi's triumph as a *chawala* boy becoming the PM fits the bill.

The current regime is in place to rapidly subsume any and all citizens' rights at a faster pace than what the UPA could manage. Assurances of rapid environmental clearances for mega projects, weakening safeguards in the Land Acquisition Act, withdrawal of the Gram Sabha's right to decide the fate of mega projects by the Ministry of Environments and Forests, handing over large tracts of forest land to corporates like Adani, amending the Coastal Regulation Zone to allow coastal lands to fall into the hands of builders, promoting the production of petrol and diesel-driven consumer cars and expanding the already vast expensive network of highways and flyovers, increasing the Foreign Direct Investment in Defence and Retail, accompanied by the dismantling of elements of welfare like the withdrawal of free medicines in Maharashtra mainly two days after the new BJP government is sworn in and the alarmingly high rate of malnutrition in the model State of Gujarat—these are a few symptoms of a phenomenon reminiscent of the close embrace between Hitler's Germany and the mega-business of his day."

It will be around a year shortly when these observations are shared with the wider public and looking back, one can see the new pace acquired by the government in implementing those policies which further marginalise the already marginalised and poor.

Gone are the days when the 2002 riots and the growing normalisation of brutality had infuriated a section of the leading capitalists who had expressed their disapproval of the ambience in the state. Today, as everyone can see, all of them have fallen in line and there is complete change in the scene. A recap of statements issued by leaders of industry then would rather seem unbelievable today. Here is an example which is worth sharing:

> What is happening there and the way the situation is being handled is definitely not right. These kinds of things are bound to have a negative impact on investment climate in Gujarat and the country as a whole.
>
> —Sanjiv Goenka, President, Confederation of Indian Industries quoted in a report, 'Industry hurt but does not moan' in *The Asian Age*, April 4, 2002

> Internationally, we have lost our name as a secular country. I am ashamed to have seen this in our country. The chief minister must take responsibility and resign. If the powers in Delhi are supporting him, it is unacceptable. If politicians have prevented the police from doing their duties, it cannot be tolerated. Some heads have to roll.
>
> — Deepak Parekh, Chairman HDFC and an industry leader in *The Times of India*, March 26, 2002

All that is *passe*.

There is no denying the fact that the corporates must be feeling vindicated that they made a right choice when they decided to project Modi as the future PM way back in 2009 itself when the Western world had closed their doors before him or investigations were on under a Special Investigating Team constituted under the directions of the Supreme Court to look into his alleged role in the infamous carnage of 2002.

In his write-up 'How Mr. Modi's voodoo economics will twist India's destiny', Prof Amitabh Bhattacharya writes:

> "...[T]oday the country can "rightfully" qualify for the dubious distinction of having the biggest divide between the haves and have-nots. While a sizeable number of Indians belong to the group of India's richest individuals the country is also home to the world's largest number of most impoverished people.
>
> Owners of capital are creating wealth for themselves at a much faster rate than the growth of the economy. Without any progressive wealth tax, the economic inequality in India is obviously set to increase even faster. The Modi government even removed wealth tax in the 2015-16 budget..."

Rise, and further rise of Gautam Adani, is rather symptomatic of the closeness of the corporate honchos to the government. Perhaps it is for the first time in independent India's around seventy years' journey that a particular corporate leader seems to be accompanying the PM on every foreign trip.

"In New York Adani sat in the audience as Modi addressed the United Nations, and he visited Japan, Australia and France at the same time as the Prime Minister. He was with the Prime Minister in Brazil, according to the *Hindustan Times* and he visited Britain with Modi according to World Trade Scanner. The compnay denied both news reports.

Adani, 52 has travelled with Modi more than any other billionaire, helping him emerge as the most prominent face of India Inc to the outer world. His wealth has more than quadrupled since Modi announced his candidacy in September 2013, the biggest gain among the country's elite.

(http;//www. bloomberg.com/news/articles/2015-0.1-27/meet-the-billionaire-trotting -the -globe-with-indian-leader-modi)

Gone also are the days when a section of the RSS leadership led by the likes of Dattoapant Thegadi had played 'spoil -sport' during the NDA-1 regime led by Vajpayee under the vague Swadeshi concerns. Today, under a new leadership, the RSS has decided to support the same policies which it had earlier opposed—which would further marginalise the already exploited, oppressed—in return for a promise that they would like the government to move ahead on their cultural agenda. One very well knows that cultural agenda is another euphemism for carving out a Hindu Rashtra out of a pluralistic/secular/democratic India.

For lay persons, the unfolding picture is somewhat difficult to comprehend where yesterday's 'Swadeshi'-loving *Pracharaks* and *Swayamsevaks* have turned into master salespersons to showcase India and are busy giving red carpet treatment to *desi-videsi* corporates. The BJP which had maintained a strange ambivalence about the economic policies of the government when in opposition is rushing to embrace them projecting to the outside world that they had been the original liberalisers. It is also incomprehensible to the ordinary people how the corporate bosses of the country and from outside are ready to digest peddling of mythology as science and history.

In fact, as far as corporate interests are concerned, which today manifest themselves in the model of neoliberalism unfolding here fascination for Hindu nationalism, Hindutva or similar exclusive ideologies is merely coincidental. The primary concern is to serve the logic of capital which subsists on profits. To put it bluntly, neoliberalism which is basically 'capitalism with its gloves off 'has demonstrated that it has tremendous flexibility and can operate under a spectrum of circumstances ranging from a monarchy to a model of liberal democracy. History bears witness to the fact that Chile's dictator Pinochet executed it through coercive violence—which was the first 'great experiment at neoliberal state formation' whereas Margaret Thatcher achieved it through the organisation of democratic consent.

(November 15-21, 2015)

8

The Discourse of Non-Violence in Indian Politics

T. Vijayendra

This essay is addressed to political activists who are on the side of the poor. At present, the poor are engaged in several major struggles and tendencies. The issue of violence and non-violence is often raised and sometimes this divides the people's movements. The aim of the article is to clarify these issues, encourage healthy debate and avoid splits in the people's movements. For the purpose of this article, the meaning of the word 'violence' is restricted only to human beings wreaking violence on other human beings. Killing animals for food is excluded. In truth, the massive destruction of flora, fauna and ecology for the explicit purpose of reducing the enemy's food supply and livelihood base should also be considered as violence.

The two great religions that have advocated non-violence are Buddhism and Christianity. One must separate the religions from the lives of their founders. Buddhism became a religion during Emperor Ashoka's (304-232 BC) time and Christianity became a religion in 380 AD during the Roman Empire under Theodosius 1 (378-395).

Now a state is an instrument of the ruling class meant to serve its interests and keep the ruled classes under control. The control is rarely done by force although the threat is always present. Most of the time however, this control is exercised through a set of cultural processes which legitimise and justify the system of state power. Religion is one of the most important among these processes. Religions ask people to be ethical and good while allowing the ruling class to continue with exploitation and oppression. The theory of non-violence has played a crucial role in this process. It disarms the people, while allowing the state and the ruling class to remain armed and use violence.

For example, Emperor Ashoka is reported to have been struck with remorse after the brutal victory in Kalinga, and then adopted Buddhism as a state religion and spread the message of Buddha. But he did not disband his army. In the year 185 BC, about fifty years after Ashoka's death, the last Maurya ruler Brahadratha, was assassinated by the commander-in-chief of the Mauryan armed forces, Pushyamitra Sunga, while taking the Guard of Honour of his forces. During Ashoka's regime, the relations between the state and religious organisations also became institutionalised. The king was anointed by the religious organisations. He, in turn, supported them through land grants and financial backing. Religions provided legitimacy to the king and the state, and asked them to be ethical. As a rule, they were on the king's side whenever the king punished the 'guilty' or waged war. Buddhism died in India around the 8th century AD but spread to Nepal, Sri Lanka, Southeast Asia, China and Japan. The Chinese and Japanese even developed 'non-violent' or 'unarmed' martial arts in self-defence in the Buddhist tradition. Today these techniques are used for police training all over the world to punish protesters or even kill them without anybody being able to prove violence. Nor did Buddhism prevent the rulers of China and Japan from having armies and waging wars. The Japanese fascists were also known for extremely brutal practices in the Second World War.

Before the Roman Empire adopted Christianity as its official religion, it would persecute Christians. Adoption of Christianity did not prevent any Christian king or emperor from having armies or waging wars. In fact the Crusades were carried out in the name of Christianity. A firm symbiotic relationship existed between the church and the king/emperor. Even with those within the religion and the Catholic Church were extremely cruel in punishing people who differed from the official version.

Modern Period

In the modern period, however, this theory has also helped the people. But, particularly in the case of Gandhi, the matter was not so simple. The three great names among the modern votaries of non-violence are Thoreau, Tolstoy and Bertrand Russell. Thoreau (1817-1862)'s 'Civil Disobedience' has inspired generations of peace activists. Leo Tolstoy (1828-1910) was very upset by the practice of Christianity by the churches and the churches' support to governments in their war efforts. For years he consistently wrote inspiring articles and books on the issue and inspired generations of people including Gandhi. He also consistently protested against Czarism in Russia and helped many revolutionaries in their cause. Lenin paid glowing tributes to Tolstoy. Tolstoy maintained that violence by the state was cold-blooded murder since it was carried out by paid functionaries. He had a different position about violence among the people. He maintained that it was not known under what provocation this violence was carried out and so one could not condemn it outright. Bertrand Russell, mathematician philosopher and pacifist, was a consistent anti-war activist. He was a campaigner against nuclear weapons and for disarmament and also a vocal critic of the US war in Vietnam. He belongs to the secular trend in the non-violence movement.

Pacifism

The secular proponents of non-violence call themselves pacifists. They oppose wars and call for disarmament. Pacifism covers a spectrum of views, including the belief that international disputes can and should be peacefully resolved. It calls for the abolition of the institutions of the military and war, opposes any organisation of society through governmental force. It rejects the use of physical violence to realise political, economic and social goals, and aims for the obliteration of force except in cases where it is absolutely necessary to advance the cause of peace. It is firm in its opposition to violence under any circumstances even for the defence of self and others.

All non-violent resistance is by no means based on a fundamental rejection of all violence in all circumstances. Many leaders and participants in such movements, while recognising the importance of using non-violent methods in particular circumstances, have not been absolute pacifists. The interconnections between civil resistance and the use of force are numerous and complex. In contrast to the principle of non-violence stands the non-aggressive principle which rejects the initiation of violence, but permits the use of it for self-defence. So it does not apply when someone is subject to violence initiated by others and hence self-defence is not morally rejected.

Proponents of Violence

There are not many articulate proponents of violence. Most of the proponents of violence in modern history have been right-wing fascists and religious fundamentalists. Today this is even more so. There are Hindu fundamentalists who carried out a mass killing of Muslims in Gujarat, the Christian fundamentalists who mowed down 80 children in a school in Norway or the Jihadis among the Muslim fundamentalists who killed hundreds of innocent people at a railway station in Mumbai.

Are Marxists Proponents of Violence?

The Marxists are also generally considered to be proponents of violence and are supposed to believe in violence as 'a means to an end'. It is however difficult to demonstrate the truth of this statement. The slogan of the Russian Revolution was 'Peace and Bread'. Communist countries took initiatives in the peace and disarmament movements. In non-Communist countries too there have always been significant numbers of Marxists in support of these movements. Their programme is a revolutionary programme for social change towards equality and the end of exploitation of man by man. Violence per se is not their programme. They accept that revolutions engender violence but by no means do they propagate it or theorise its virtues. The most familiar argument for violence is 'Violence is the midwife of revolution' where violence is compared to the necessary pain experienced by a mother during childbirth. But it would appear that Marxists are considered violent by default because they do not propagate non-violence or because they do not agree that the state has a monopoly of violence.

There is however a real problem of sectarian and fratricidal violence among the revolutionaries and communists. It has existed from the beginning but it reached a large scale during the Stalinist era in the Soviet Union. Votaries of non-violence normally cite this to say that violence per se is wrong and can never bring any social change and will always bring a new ruling class. Communists treat this as a problem that has to be worked upon. They see it more as a problem of correctly organising and leading the movement and resolving the problem of democracy and debate within the movement.

However in Indian politics, the Marxists and Communists have been dubbed as believers in violence and condemned by the so-called votaries of non-violence. This was, and still is, an attempt to hide the agenda of class collaboration and oppose the communist agenda of class struggle.

Franz Fanon

If one wants to find a theoretician of violence in left-wing politics, it was Franz Fanon (1925-1961) who wrote the book *The Wretched of the Earth*. It was published shortly before Fanon's death in 1961. Fanon defends the rights of a colonised people to use violence in their struggle for independence. His argument is that colonisers in Africa do not consider the colonised Africans as human beings. Therefore such human beings—who are not considered as human beings—shall not be bound by the principles that apply to humanity. Fanon's book was censored by the French government.

He was a psychologist with the French Army in Algeria. He had the unenviable task of counselling French soldiers who were torturing Algerian revolutionaries. The soldiers could not sleep well and had disturbing dreams. The book is a powerful description of colonialism and how the colonialists do not recognise the blacks as human beings at all. It describes how racism is constructed. Fanon also describes how a black African internalises this low estimate of himself and how violence plays a role in liberating him, how it gives him courage to revolt against the white colonialist. When the black man raises his head he finds that the white man is not any bigger than him in size. When a black man hits the white man and draws blood and sees fear in his eyes—that is the point when he realises that he can revolt against the colonialist and win! Violence is liberating! He receives a baptism of blood!

Fanon's exhortations to violence can be seen in these quotes: "For in the first phase killing is a necessity; killing a European is killing two birds with one stone eliminating at one go the oppressor and oppressed; leaving one man dead and the other man free." And "Violence is man recreating himself."

Non-Violence in India

While there will be a critique of Gandhi, it needs to be stated that there is a difference between what Gandhi thought and said and what his followers interpreted it to mean. Also, actions often lead to results different from what the proponents say or mean. The story begins with the publication of *Hind Swaraj* in 1908. It is an important book and even after 100 years of its publication it is still available in print in several languages and is still being discussed. It is a curious document. At one level it presents a dream of India which resonates with today's ideas of a post-fossil fuel era, along with reducing the scale of energy use and working towards ecological restoration. At another level it announces Gandhi's arrival in Indian politics after his success in South Africa and lays out his agenda which was different from the existing agenda of other politicians seeking independence. The book's main aim however was to isolate the revolutionaries who, according to Gandhi believed in violence. This was because Gandhi believed that the independence struggle should be fought by non-violent means and that means and ends cannot be different. The tone of the book is paternalistic and Gandhi chides the supporters of these revolutionaries. This was Gandhi's manifesto.

Very few believed his manifesto wholly, and most of his followers in the independence movement supported and used his method of non-violence tactically. The irony was that independence was not achieved without violence. Up to a million people died in communal riots during a few months. No revolution in history was so violent.

Gandhi himself was aware of this contradiction and was deeply anguished by it. "Gandhi's anguish was centred around the tragic discovery that the freedom struggle led by him had not been the unique non-violent struggle that he and the whole world believed it to have been. The discovery forced itself upon when the country erupted into savage violence on the eve of independence." (Sudhir Chandra: *Gandhi: Rethinking the Possibility of Non-Violence,* CSSS, Surat, 2012)

Gandhi's Critics

Gandhi was opposed by large sections of freedom fighters. Some opposed him openly while others were opposed to him but used him and his methods to serve their own agenda. In fact, except for a few, almost all his supporters even within the Congress party were 'opportunistic' supporters with their own agenda. Many of his Congress supporters looked forward to forming the government in New India.

One critique of Gandhi runs as follows. Unlike his *guru,* Tolstoy, Gandhi was not consistent in his practice of non-violence. Even after the publication of *Hind Swaraj,* he recruited soldiers for Britain in the First World War. He did not condemn state violence, and did not ask Indian soldiers to resign from the army though he asked Indian students to leave schools and colleges. When some Indian soldiers refused to fire at an armed Indian people's protest, Gandhi did not defend the soldiers but said that they should have the moral courage to bear the punishment of their defiance of authority.

According to some, Gandhi succeeded because of one fatal flaw in his theory: the theory of trusteeship. Trusteeship meant that the rich could keep their wealth but should act as its trustee. Many of his colleagues pointed out the contradiction between this doctrine and that of non-accumulation. The doctrine gave him the support of the Indian bourgeoisie and ensured complete press coverage of the point of view because the bourgeoisie controlled the press. As Arundhati Roy has observed, Gandhi's methods were like theatre; they required an audience. Many critics also pointed out that without a 'free press', Gandhi's methods could not succeed. The Indian bourgeoisie supported Gandhi, welcomed him into their homes and donated land and money. After the Second World War, when their purpose was served and it became clear that they would inherit the country, Gandhi was completely dropped by them.

The Indian bourgeoisie supported Gandhi not because he had an ideology of trusteeship. They saw that Gandhi was opposed to the communists and was able to perform the magic of mass mobilisation while appearing as the messiah of the poor. They saw Gandhi's methods as the road to the smooth transition of power from the British to the Indian bourgeoisie. Gandhi's agenda also successfully isolated the communists. Only a part of the socialist movement had veered towards communism and there has been a bitter struggle between the socialists and communists ever since.

Some critics say that the issue was never between violence and non-violence, for no one was advocating violence per se. The issue was independence with social justice or independence with the brown bourgeoisie replacing the white. To them, Gandhi's agenda appeared clearly for the latter (although Gandhi was very concerned about injustice in the Hindu society towards the lower castes). As events proved, the bourgeois agenda succeeded. If anything, the logic of his policies facilitated such an agenda.

Finally, some say that Gandhi's disourse on non-violence was deeply religious asking people to disarm and to be ethical, and that this legitimised the violence of the ruling classes.

Post-Independence India

Post-independence India continued to harp on how India won independence through non-violent means even while the huge shadow of a million deaths during the partition hung over it. Also there was not a single day till today when the Indian state has not been at war with some sections of the Indian people. Gandhi's legacy, such as it was passed over to Vinoba Bhave. These people did not oppose any injustice done by the Indian state. Whatever little militancy Gandhi had was completely blurred by Vinoba and his ilk.

Both the Indian state and Vinoba Bhave continued the Gandhian tradition of isolating the Left by calling them believers in violence. Vinoba started his Bhoodan movement in Telangana explicitly to oppose the communists. In 1967, Jayaprakash Narayan, another of these Gandhians, went to Musahari to oppose the Naxalites. Both of them had no success.

Today a hundred fires are burning against the Indian state. There are the CPI(Maoist)-led movements which engulf more than 100 districts of India; there are identrity movements in the North-East, Kashmir and several Indian states, notably Darjeeling and Vidarbha. There anti mega-project movements by peasants and rural people whose livelihood is endangered by these projects and which are also environmental hazards. In most of these cases, at some stage the state opposes them violently often killing several people. It also harasses the so-called 'non-violent' people through the police and judiciary. And all the time it calls for using democratic means and exhorts people to give up violence. Thus the most violent people are calling upon others to become non-violent.

The most blatant case is the case of violence in Chhattisgarh. The state created a vigilante army named *Salwa Julum* with the express purpose of fighting the Maoists. The real purpose of the state was to get land for the industry by displacing the tribals. More than a lakh of tribals were driven out of the area to Andhra Pradesh. The state has been repeatedly exposed by the press, civil liberty organisations, Gandhians like Himangsu Kumar, scholars and finally by the Supreme Court.

To sum up, the discourse on non-violence is mainly used to isolate the forces that are fighting for the people, by labelling them violent and undemocratic and dividing the movement. The proponents are by and large those who unleash violence on the people. Yet there are people who fall into this trap and start criticising the Left and the Maoists. It should be noted that many other advocates of non-violence are actually fighting for the poor, whereas those who are (Gandhians like Himangshu Kumar in Chhattisgarh and earlier Man Mohan Chaudhury in Orissa) usually avoid getting into this debate.

Conclusions

Violence exists because people live in a class-divided society where the ruling class rules with the help of the state. The state employs violence, using its standing army armed police and store of arms to keep the ruled classes under control. The state is the primary source of violence in society.

Violence is undoubtedly evil and every effort should be made by all to minimise and ultimately eliminate it. However in Indian politics, the discourse of non-violence is used to disarm the people and divide the people's movement while allowing the state and the ruling class to remain unarmed. It labels the politics of class struggle as violence and hides the politics of class collaboration under the garb of non-violence. Its aim is to isolate the socialists and communists and condemn them as believers in violence. The discourse of violence and non-violence in Indian politics is, therefore a false discourse. It is a bourgeois agenda. The way out is to firmly oppose the state and ruling class by uniting all opposition. Those who want to use peaceful means should use the secular discourse of peaceful democratic means of struggle. There is scope for plurality of approaches. But there is no scope for this false discourse of violence and non-violence.

(Autumn Number 2014)

9

From the Last Dancer

Gayatri Chakravorty Spivak

Edward W. Said died in 2003. Jacques Derrida died in 2004. Kofi Awoonor was killed in West Gate Mall last year. Now Stuart Hall is gone. And Ernesto Laclau. A generation of intellectuals and activists intellectual/activists, is disappearing.

Academics worldwide could not think of "Black Britain" before Stuart Hall. And, in Britain, the impact of Cultural Studies went beyond the confines of the academy. That quiet, gentle, learned, witty, tenacious original political thinker inspired generations of students into intellectual and cultural production that spilled over into hands-on activism. Paul Gilroy, Angela McRobbie, Issac Julien, Michelle Barret, John Akomfrah, the list goes on.

It was my good fortune to meet Stuart Hall with an opportunity of spending quality time with him in discussion at the Marxist Cultural Interpretation Institute in Champaign-Urbana in 1983, under the shadow of Shabra and Shatila. Stuart Hall recounted the days of the saving of the *New Left Review* when the Russell Foundation no longer supported it in, if memory serves, 1963. (I was in Britain that year, a young Bengali woman tyrannised by a pre-feminist white alpha-male financially dependent resentful commpanion, a transient research student at Girton, two years out of India, not part of the radical mainstream.) Hall was among the founders in the 1950s of the *New Left Review*.

I cannot museumise Stuart in the widely claimed Euro-US

protest scenes of the 1960s, as widely claimed as the Naxalbari movement at home. He surely belonged to it as a passionate participant, even a charismatic leader, but mourning takes me elsewhere.

Today I remember that it was also the moment of the death of Lumumba, Fanon and Du Bois. In other words, Hall came in and participated without epistemic recognition, at the inauguration of a new way of thinking of the world, long-haul, not just immediate protest or resistance. I cannot confine him to a merely British cultural studies alone, even as it preserves its political difference from US Cultural Studies identitarianism betraying the austere hospitality of democracy; I read him rather in the world that worked for social justice in the diversified field of the struggle for citizenship in the metropolis after the waning of territorial imperialisms; and after the passing of the initial dreams of negritude and Pan-Africanism.

It was Awoonor who made me imagine the early 60s in the worldly way. Awoonor came back to Accra with a good Brit Lit degree from Leeds even as the New Left was consolidating itself at Oxford. Smart boy from Africa not in the British radical mainstream Awoonor became Du Bois's minder. He remembers the move against Du Bois's sympathies with a peculiar communism which meant passport denial in the United States but might mean going with the Eastern bloc in newly-fledged Ghana. (Remember Padmore's *Pan-Africanism or Communism*?[1] And that Marcus Garvy was seriously taken as an alternative? More important, he remembered the 1959 Pan-African Congress with both Lumumba and Fanon ("the tall one and the short one") in attendance. I want to place Hall, young man lately arrived from Jamaica, in this broad world for the philosophers of the future, rather than keep him local. I wish he were here for me to be having this discussion about global connectivities. You listened to Stuart Hall contradicted, but also, sometimes, agreed.

I can sense the shadow of this reconstellation in "When was the Postcolonial?"[2] Although the essay apparently relates to a debate, by now forgotten, between "postcolonial critics" and

Arif Dirlik, Ella Shohat, Anne MacClintock, Lata Mani, Ruth Frankenbubrg, Mary Louise Pratt, Robert Young, Homi Bhabha." Larger issues are 'at stake' in these debates than the criticisms which have been widely signalled sometimes suggest." (256)

Paragraph after paragraph describes—without mentioning Africa—the predicament of post-colonial nation-states in Africa, a predicament that clearly signals Africa's nationalism division into regionalism, unexamined culturalism. As we are today reeling under the dismissal of a good governor of Nigeria's Central Bank, or looking at an ageing FLN member running again for president in Algeria, tremendous ethnic conflict in Kenya, and inequitable infrastructure and education system below a certain class in Ghana—and, indeed at the well-known fact that the difference between rich and poor is most aggravated in sub-Saharan Africa with South Africa coming close behind, we read Hall's words about "the emergence of powerful local elites managing the contradictory effects of under-development.... characterised by the persistence of many of the effects of colonisation but at the same time their displacement from the coloniser/colonised axis to their internalisation within the decolonised society itself" in the context of Africa, not, as he does, in the context of the Gulf States, where we are looking at Sykes-Picot.[3] Rather do I hear Assia Djebar, in Paris/North Africa, bringing colonial and post-colonial violence together, exclaiming in October, 1988: *"Once more O Frantz the 'wretched of the earth'"*, but now it is Algerian killing Algerian.[4]

In some countries, the desired solution is to make the countries safe for foreign direct investment. This is Hall's "devil and the deep blue sea", not the contradiction in Dirlik's, or Shohat's or yet Robert Young's arguments.

It should be noticed that Hall's arguments do not apply to the proliferating examples of the removal of bad heads of state, by popular movements being signalled as "revolution" with no preparation for building new states. It is in the context of "Africa rising", looking at tradition surviving interregionally rather than favouring conflict, that we can read Hall's words about "some other, related, but as yet 'emergent' new configurations of power-knowledge relations... bgining to exert their distinctive and specific effects" (254). We can read them in the context of emerging informal markets competitive with the ruling view of the world that can no longer think of democracy."[5] "Cultural Studies" material, for analysis, not just celebration.

While the New Left was organising itself at Oxford, W.E.B. Du Bois in Ghana was looking carefully, as Marx looked at Lewis Morgan at responsible critical scholarly anthropological texts describing West, South, East Africa, making notes, marking Indexes—to combat the stupidity of declaring the Negro slave population stupid because violently withdrawn from impressively structured social organisation tremendous statistical and historical achievement inscribed on mnemic material and altogether impressive linguistic sophistication, where the line from figurative practice to rational choice was always active in daily life. (No mere romanticism of Africa this. Du Bois had no interest in denying the cruelty and absolute hierarchisation in these political formations.) He is looking to examine how post-slavery African-Americans in the American South could possiby have worked with the structural principles of Reconstruction and parliamentary administration and, if his marginalia and index markings are to be trusted, he is thinking of something operating in the absence of any entry granted into intellectual labour—something that Fernand Braudel would later call the *longue duree*—persistent perennial residual structures unrecognisable by Southern gentry and benevolent collecting types—so that we are dealing not just with exceptions such as Phyllis Wheatly and Frederick Douglass but also with the general community of emancipated slaves.

It is here that Stuart Hall's work on ideology and national identity can be made intertextual within a field that is not usually recognised as his. The work of Gilroy and Julien, in their different ways, have elaborated such possibiities. In the evenings there in Ghana, back from Du Bois I read Awoonor's posthumously published *The Promise of Hope*. There is a moving tribute there to the Jamaican activist writer Neville Augustus Dawes, a writer involved in the transformation of Pan-Africanism in postcoloniality. Stuart Hall was resolutely North London. Yet I want to close with some words from that inclusive homage because I, a New Yorker have tried to write this tribute to my friend Stuart Hall in the spirit of conjunctural inclusiveness and solidarity. There was a time when I would say I was a chick vocalist in the theory performing band—Stuart Hall, Edward Said, Fredric Jameson, Hayden White. I put here a picture from that era courtesy Rainer Ganahl.[6] And that casual often-repeated comment of mine lets me borrow the grander metaphor of the last dancer from the poem.

Am I reading him right? Who can read anyone right? I am reading him, claiming him. The editors asked us to take as "[g]iven the points of intersection between [our] thought and the work, the project of Stuart Hall. "Am I doing more than attempting to stand at one of those crossroads? In 1985 Hall warned us away from a "continuous slippage away from any conceivable conjuncture."[7] I am shifting from an embedded into an embedding conjuncture, away from his deep involvement with the British context, the CND, the disappointment over Hungary, from working class to mass culture, the Open University, to the open ocean of Du Bois's Stalinism in the face of disappointment with capitalist democracy, Lumumba's betrayal by East, West Africa; Fanon as a bridge, if you like—creating "an articulation in terms of effects which does not necessarily correspond to its origins." Put it down to my unease with Little Britain as is with "post-structuralism". Standing on the crossroads, I am grasping at the retractable moments.[8]

In "What is This 'Black' in Black Popular Culture," Hall invokes a shift from the Euro-US and speaks of the diaspora. But what of a "global" Nigerian dreams of a different Kingston? It will not be as Hall says somewhere, reggae, and canned fruit raining down from coconut palms. Allow me, then

> *I come again I say half-clansman of the ritual goat*
> *tethered to a forgotten tree*
> *in a ruined and alien field; I am the last dancer in the circular*
> *team kicking only dust after the graceful ones are done*

the jeers and sneers echoing
down the vast saharas of my history
on whose corner
this day, this natal day,
I weep anew
for historical follies I could not shed
abilities I did not realise
victories I did not savour, hopes I did not endure.[9]

When I heard of Stuart Hall's death, I was in Calcutta writing a piece on Coleridge where I was discovering when the postcolonial was.[10]

REFERENCES

1. George Padmore, *Pan-Africanism or Communism? The Coming Struggle for Africa* (New York: Roy Publishers, 1956).
2. Stuart Hall, "When was the post-colonial thinking at the Limit?" in Ian Chamber and Lidia Curti, eds., *The Post Colonial Question* (New York, Routledge, 1996)
3. I refer to the Sykes-Picot agreement—between the French and the British—that carved out boundaries of separate states—breaking promises earlier made with Arab muftis—in the Middle East in 1917.This was part of the de-Ottomanisation undertaken at the collapse of the Ottoman Empire in the early 20th century by European powers. It can be argued that this de-Ottomanisation displaced an earlier conflict with the holy Roman Empire and continues to this day. That today's Middle Eastern conflict against what is perceived as an Israel-United States combination has retained this as cultural memory is reflected, for example, as an apparent dissolving of the boundaries between Syria and Iraq in ISIS (The Islamic State of Iraq and Syria), with its allegiance to a Caliph. "Their (the leaders of ISIS) stated goal is to obliterate the Middle-Eastern borders drawn as spheres of influence by Western colonial powers after the First World War. They aim to undo the partitioning of Muslim lands by Crusader powers." (Francis X Clines, "ISIS Storms the Barricades, Justices Unite and Republicans Sing", *New York Times*, 6/29/14 p. SR 2). This is a different configuration from the effects of the absence of the practice of freedom under colonialism in literally post-colonial new nations.

4. Aqssia Djebar, *Algerian White: A Narrative in David Kelley and Marjolijn de Jaeger* (New York: Seven Stories, 2000), p. 92. The problem in South Asian postcoloniality is related, but also differently organised by the *longue duree* of the caste system morphing itself into a unique Islamophobia that is distinguishable from the international variety taking us back to Sykes-Picot. Although the practice of freedom is not accessible to any colony, South Asia is determined by a different style of European imperial policy.
5. Dayo Olopade, *The Bright Continent–Breaking Rules and Making Changes in Modern Africa* (New York: Houghton Mifflin 2014).
6. Rainer Ganahl, *Seminar/Lecture, Teresa de Lauretis, Stuart Hall, Gayatri Chakravorty Spivak, Moderator Mark Nash, Conditions of Identification, Questions of Difference,* New York, 19/12/96.
7. Hall, "Signification Representation, Ideology: Althusser and the Post-Structuralist Debates," *Critical Studies in Mass Communication* 2 (1985), pp. 92-93, 95.
8. "How is the refraction of existence in the ideological sign determined? By an intersection"—my crossroads—"of differently interested social interests, in every ideological sign" (Volosinov quoted in Hall," Rediscovery of 'Ideology': Return of the Repressed in Media Studies" in Michael Gurevitch et al. eds, *Culture, Society and the Media* (New York, Methuen, 1982), p. 79.
9. Koli Awoonor, "In Memoriam: Return to Kingston" in *The Promise of Hope: New and Selected Poems, 1964-2013* (Lincoln: University of Nebraska Press, 2014), p. 76.
10. "Willing Suspension of Disbelief, Here, Now," forthcoming in Forest Pyle III, ed. *Constellations of Contemporary Romanticism* (New York: Fordham University Press).

10

Stop the War

Jan Myrdal

[A slightly abridged version of a speech delivered by the author at a seminar to express solidarity with the struggling people of Kashmir and Palestine at Brighton on June 29, 2013.]

Palestine and Kashmir are both under military occupation. In both cases this occupation and the periodically violent conflict with the security forces has been going on for more than sixty years. The history of popular solidarity work in metropolitan and other states with people suffering under colonial and imperialist rule is of course much longer.

Solidarity is not a question of doing something for others. This is not a truth just for the present. You know the words of John Donne from 1624: "No man is an island...." Well, Marx in the 19th century pointed out that the struggle against the oppression of the Irish is necessary for the liberation here in Britain. But there is a difference between the social and political work we take part in directly, you in the UK and we in Sweden, and our solidarity work. The solidarity work has a different agenda. I as a Swede must understand that it is not for me to say how the struggle for liberation in Palestine and Kashmir is to be conducted. I might have opinions. That is another thing. But the decision of how to struggle is not for me.

Nearly two generations ago, we built a Swedish mass movement for solidarity with the people of Southeast Asia in their national struggle against French colonialism and the

United States war. We did it independently and from below, outside parties. We expressed our principle of solidarity to the representatives of Southeast Asia as "solidarity on your terms." It was for them—not us to decide.Why did we express ourselves in this way? We had summed up the experience of anti-colonial and anti-imperial and peace movements the last more than hundred years! Those of you who are from South Asia know the detrimental effects of well meaning outside advice and interference during the liberation struggle in the 1930s and 40s.

During the first years, the solidarity work against the United States war in Southeast Asia was an uphill struggle. Not only were the mass media against us. Militants lost their jobs, both the security police and the regular police were used against us. Towards the end of 1967, the government even—for the first time in Sweden since 1917—had set in mounted police against our peaceful demonstration. I too was beaten up, jailed and given a four-year jail sentence. But we had at that time such a strong following that the government changed policies. If you can't beat them—join them! And in the next demonstration, Olof Palme, then minister for education, later prime minister, led the demonstration. Of course, the United States government was furious at Sweden. Our movement had by keeping a principle line and through talking to people selling bulletins, demonstrating and holding meetings grown to a mass movement and thus been instrumental in changing the official Swedish policies, which was good for our own independence as a nation.

Twelve years before my birth, Norway fought for independence from the union with Sweden. What I could call "we" in Sweden, the labour movement and the socialist youth league, were not only active but were a determining force in stopping the ruling class in Sweden from going to war with Norway. The leader of the Swedish Social Democracy, Hjalmar Branting, was sentenced in 1895 for warning the government that their policy could result in "a bullet" against them or those responsible for war. Ten years later when the crisis became acute, the socialist youth league spread the word among the recruits of our conscript army that in case of war against Norway, they should turn their guns in the right direction; the officers of the Swedish army had to be sought before they could give any orders. The open threat of civil war scared the ruling class and it did not choose war but let Norway go. But remember—these I rightly can call "we" did not interfere in Norwegian affairs. They surely were not in favour of the Norwegians opting for monarchy, for instance. But that was a decision only for the Norwegians.

As we all know, or should be aware of, the freedom of the media in countries of our type will be restricted when the dominant forces deem it in their interest. The gate keepers of the official media earn their pay by keeping the public misinformed. But still it is normally in our countries not in the strict sense illegal to spread information that is being kept out of the media. Thus the solidarity work to a large extent becomes supplying basic information. I don't think ordinary people in this country have a clear understanding even of the great crime in Palestine 65 years ago: Al nakba. Then 75,000 Palestinians were driven from their land upon which the state of Israel then was erected and evicted Palestinians forcibly, at gun point, forbidden ever to return.

This crime is continuing as settlers, many of them coming from Sweden or the United States or Eastern Europe, contrary to all international law, build their villages on Palestinian land that was occupied by Israeli forces in the last violent annexation campaign. They try to sell the products of this illegally occupied land in our countries. In Sweden, we agitate against this. Inform, demonstrate. Show that the managers of the food chains selling this are in fact receivers of stolen goods.

Now and then governments and politicians from the United Kingdom, the United States and others of our countries mutter. But they do not stop the Israelis. The reason is clear; if you go back to the First World War, you find that the present policies supporting the state of Israel are a continuation of that economic and military Great Game in West and Central Asia. This truth has to be clarified in order to gain popular support in our countries for the freedom struggle of the Palestinian people.

At times there have in fact been attempts through the United States to reach a solution that was not a continuing crime against the Palestinian people. But when the Swedish count Bernadotte came forward with such a plan then Yizak Shamir—who later became prime minister of the Israeli state—just had him murdered.It is important for us in Sweden to keep makig thins murder known. Pro-Israeli groups have after the murder tried to slander him as pro-Nazi. He was not. He was a normal member of the royal family, not a revolutionary but as the head of the Swedish Red Cross he managed at the end of the war to get Himmler to let at least Scandinavian prisoners out of the German concentration camps. He saved some 15,000 prisoners from different countries. He was murdered on September 17, 1948 as he was putting forward a solution that went against the plan of the extreme Zionists.

This murder was swept under the carpet. As far as the governments of what was called "the west" are concerned, there will be no reactions against the continuous crimes of the Israeli state against the Palestinian people, if we are not able to organise and put such an internal pressure on them that they have to act.

Here we must be able to see clearly with whom can we cooperate in this work. Let me take an example. In the 1950s, during the beginning of the war for national liberation in Algeria, I lived in Paris. Who supported the Algerian people in their struggle? Not the big and then still officially revolutionary labour movement and their notables. It was small ultra-left groups as the FCL, "Federation communiste libertaire" and the PCI, "Parti communiste internationaliste", a Catholic writer, member of the French Academy who had just received the Nobel Prize, Francois Mauriac and then different writers and intellectuals generally. There are reasons for this. I can discuss them another time. But the pattern is the same today in the very broad solidarity movement with Palestine in Sweden. Several Christian organisations, many of them inside the Swedish Church are from a humanitarian stand, very active supporters of the Palestinian people and their rights. Yes, allies in the solidarity work can often be found in unexpected places. Or, as Fidel Castro said when I was in Cuba in 1967 making a film: "A Catholic priest taking a stand from the rights of the poor and oppressed is a friend of the people, whereas an officially communist party that stands aside is not."

It is also necessary to closely watch the contradictions among the ruling classes. That the Swedish government of that time early on made contact with the Algerian liberation movement and then also as a first state established diplomatic relations with Algeria was important.

(Autumn Number, 2013)

11

In Memory of Abhijit Roy of Religion and Marxism

Aloke Mukherjee

On February 26, 2015, a group of religious bigots killed Abhijit Ray, a rationalist blogger, for his opposition to religious obscurantism. The incident took place in Dacca. No person with some degree of conscience can look upon such a horrific act by an organised group as condonable. While condemning the killing and pledging to fight out such forces, we have to face a concrete question, the question of combating these killer groups in the name of religion and bringing the people out of the quagmire of religion, which was the mission of Abhijit Roy.

With the exception of one Hindu (Brahminical, to be exact) religious text, namely the *Bhagavad Gita*, no single text of any religion, be it Hindu, Islam, Christian or any other, teaches people to kill others in order to preserve or save religion, *dharma*. But there had taken place and still are taking place killings, conflicts, wars, progroms, riots and attacks on ordinary people—all in the name of religion—in different parts of the world. After that event of 11 September, the US President gave the call for a crusade, "a war between two civilisations". There was opposition throughout the world against this statement, but very few cared to call it an act of terror or instigation to terror and nobody branded it as Christian fundamentalism (whatever that term might mean), though it was a clear and unambiguous attempt to rally the Christians of the world behind the imperialist design of the US to carry on its war in the Middle East in the name of fighting Islamic terrorism.

Against this backdrop, real methods and strategies for combating the use of religion in the interests of a few, and for abolition of religion should be drawn, be it in the USA or in India or Bangladesh or elsewhere in the world. The best strategy so far was laid down more than one century ago by Karl Marx. But the tragedy is that most of the Marxists, especially in this subcontinent, never tried to understand it, let alone act accordingly. As a result, a single phrase of Marx was quoted without context. "It (religion) is the opium of the people." And they started asking people to get rid of this 'opium', going to the extent of sermonising. But if we look at the paragraph itself (the context of this paragraph will be discussed later), we shall find what Marx actually meant. He said, "Religious suffering is at the same time an expression of real suffering and a protest against real suffering. Religion is the sigh of the oppressed creatures, the sentiment of a heartless world, and soul of soulless conditions. It is the opium of the people." [Karl Marx, *Selected Writings in Sociology and Social Philosophy*, (ed) T.B. Bottomore and Maximillan Rubel, p. 41]

Here a Marxist worth his salt should differ from rationalists (both of idealist and mechanical varieties) in that people's faith in religion does not grow just from a subjective understanding of the world, but does have a real basis in the real world. We may quote what Marx, just before penning the sentences quoted above, said about the "making of religion". "Man makes religion, religion does not make man. Religion is indeed man's self-consciousness and self-awareness as long as he has not found his feet in this universe. But man is not an abstract being, squatting outside this world. Man is the world of men, the State and society. This State, this society, produces religion, which is an inverted world consciousness, because they are an inverted world. Religion is the general thory of this world, its encyclopaedic compendium, its logic in popular form, its spiritual point *d'honneur*, its enthusiasm, its moral sanction, its solemn complement, its general basis of consolation and justification. It is the fantastic realisation of the human being as long as the human being possesses no true reality. The struggle against religion is therefore indirectly a struggle against that world whose spiritual aroma is religion." (Ibid., p. 41)

In the present world, imperialists and their cohorts running the states also use religion for their own purposes. They need religion to keep the people in a state of passivity, to keep them from acting against this real world of oppression and suppression facing them at each and every moment and to fall back upon a Supreme Being for amelioration. On the other hand, those who are vying for power without any qualitative change in the state and the society try to use religion as a means to rally the people behind them. Sometimes a few non-state actors, as in the case of the killers of Abhijit Roy, use terrorist activities in the name of religion in order to pave the way for either of the contending parties vying for power. In some cases, they act for either of two belligerent states fighting each other.

So far about the making of religion, how and why people fall back upon religion and also how this is used by the state, the existing society. But the point is how to change the condition, how to create a situation where people would not feel the need to fall back upon religion. Can it be done by explaining that no superstructural being does exist? Can it be done by demonstrating how hydrogen and oxygen, combined in definite quantities in a definite condition, produce water? Yes, a small section either placed in an opportune position in society or having highly developed consciousness about nature and society will understand it. To that extent, such a rational approach will succeed, and that is certainly an achievement. For the majority of the people, however, it would not work, the reason being that because of the conditions under which they live, they need their consolation in the illusion of religion. So it will not be sufficient to abolish religion, and for that matter, the bigotry of those vested interests who need religion for their benefit.

In this context, Marx said, "The abolition of religion as the illusory happiness of men is a demand for their real happinness.

The call to abandon their illusions about their conditions is a call to abandon conditions which require illusions." (Ibid., pp. 41-42)

This means creation of a society where there would be no exploitation, oppression or suppression of men by men, people would be happy to live a life of their own choice by working according to their ability for the society and getting what they need from the society.

This is the goal we have to reach for complete abolition of religion. To reach that goal certain tasks must be fulfilled, certain immediate tasks have to be undertaken. On that also Marx had the following to say:

"The immediate task is to unmask human alienation in its secular form, not that it is unmasked in its sacred form. Thus the criticism of heaven transcends itself to criticism of earth, the criticism of religion into the criticism of law, and criticism of theology into the criticism of politics."(Ibid., p. 42)

Thus real steps towards abolition of religion can only be to change the world around us. Without a concrete practice to change the state and society, which are based on an unjust relationship between man and man, all efforts to abolish religion will not only fail, but may even become counterproductive. That is why just a call to abandon religion cannot motivate people to do so. Rather those who try to do that either get alienated froom the people or unwillingly become pawns in the hands of powers-that-be. That is why a section of them, getting frustrated, become members of the puja committes or go to Tarapith in the name of integration with the people. That is why the US imperialists often reward a section of rationalists for their criticism of Islam. That is why the RSS circulated pirated copies of *Lajja* by Taslima Nasrin, when it was proscribed. Moreover, we also find persons who, instead of calling the people to combat the religious bigots who killed Abhijit Roy, appeal to the state to punish the killers and lament that had the state punished the killers of Humayun Azad earlier, such acts would not have been repeated.

The task is simple but difficult. It is simple because instead of any abstract idea, there is a concrete solution before us. "The religious reflection of the real world can, in any case, only finally vanish when practical relations of everyday life offer to man none but perfectly intelligible and reasonable conditions to his fellowmen and to nature." (Marx, *Capital,* Vol. 1, p. 84)

In order to get out of the present irrational world, and to reach "perfectly intelligible and reasonable conditions", the people will have to get rid of this exploitative and oppressive system. So the call to the people should make it clear that so long as the people live in a society where exploitation of man by man is the order of the day, they cannot reach a life of real happiness. It is only by changing this unjust society that the people can become masters of their own lives. And what sort of society do they need?

"The life process of society, i.e. the process of material production will not shed its mystical veil unless it beomes a product of freely associated men, and is consciously regulated by them in accordance with a settled plan. This, however, demands for society a certain material groundwork or set of conditions of existence which in their turn are the spontaneous product of a long and painful process of development." (*Capital,* Vol. 1, p. 84)

At the same time, the task is difficult. The reason is that it can be accomplished only when a society whose material production will be carried on by "freely associated men" and is "consciously regulated" by them according to "a settled plan"comes into being. This means a communist society. Such a society can evolve from the womb of a socialist society through "a long and painful process of development." But in the present world context, after the change of colour of both the USSR and China, it has become harder and more difficult.

But it is also true that the USSR and China had shown the path; they had their successes that shook the world. They had their positive and negative aspects. Positive in the sense that we had seen their great achievements. Negative in the sense that we often became blind, blindly following them and blindly supporting each and every action of them. But the failures have taught us. Endowed with experiences of both successes and failures, we are now more steeled, and as the cause is before us, we have to rise to the occasion.

Hence, in order to avenge the murder of Abhijit, let us go to the people, get integrated with the toiling masses, and share their weal and woe, be students before being teachers. Let us rally the vast masses of the people to fight out this irrational social order. Once that is done, the ugly faces of the murderers and their masters behind the scene will be unmasked and they will not be able to hide themselves behind the veil of religion. Their real character as enemies of the masses will be clear.

12

Romain Rolland's Letters to Joseph Stalin (1935-1937)

Translated by *Paresh Chattopadhyay*

[The following is a free translation of letters written to Joseph Stalin (in French) by Romain Rolland, a world figure of the early 20th century—novelist, dramatist, essayist, Nobel Prize winner in literature (1915), great humanist, anti-fascist, a friend of Rabindranath Tagore, M.K. Gandhi and Einstein among others, author of a huge novel *Jean Christophe,* musicologist and professor of the history of music at the famous Sorbonne in Paris. The present translator had the privilege of visiting his Paris house circa in 1964, where he saw two pictures on the wall, those of Rabindranath Tagore and Beethoven.

These letters were written in Russia's critical years of the mid-1930s, the time of show trials. One remarkable fact is Stalin never answered any of these letters.So the correspondence remained one-sided. Among the many points raised by Rolland, not all could be covered here; only the points considered (of course arbitrarily) relatively more important is taken up for translation.]

[October 1, 1935]

Dear Comrade Stalin,

I learn from Bukharin's letter that you have not received my letter which I had sent you by registered mail on August 26. Would you be kind enough to confirm this?

I had asked in this letter if you would authorise me to

publish in France the text of our conversation of 28th June. You will do me a favour by your response on this subject.

[December 27, 1935]

Dear Comrade

I am not sure if you have received my letters. I wrote to you two letters over the last two months, but I have not got any response. You will remember that during our conversation, I had stressed the fact that serous misunderstndings were being caused in the opinion in the West by the total absence of exact information on what was happening in the USSR, even among the friends of the USSR and this lack of precise information has stood in the way of answering the serious accusations against the USSR. You had recognised the seriousness of my observations and the need of remedying this lacuna. You had told me and I quote you "certainly, if our friends in the West are ill-informed about the motives that are behind the acts of the Soviet government, and they do not know how to respond to our enemies, that signifies also that we do not sufficiently arm our friends. We will try to correct the situation. Certainly we could react more energetically against the absurd rumours." Dear Comrade, five months have passed since you told me these things. Nothing has been done to correct the situation, and the evil has considerably increased. You cannot imagine the quantity and the seriousness of the questions that assail us—the friends of the Soviet Union—daily and which exercise the world public opinion.

It would be a dangerous error to underestimate all this and to think that if there is no response, they woud be forgotten. Since the last six months I have been witnessing an increasing disaffection for the USSR among those intellectuals whom we had earlier won over to the cause of the USSR. These people are increasingly disillusioned as they do not have answers to many disturbing questions. We, to whom they turn for exact answers, can only answer them by our own personal conviction and not by providing them with correct answers.

I shall not return to the question of publication of my conversation with you.You have not responded to my question on this subject. I shall not insist on that. But even if the publication is avoided, the questions raised on that occasion demand an urgent response which one could use countering the accusations in public.

I shall raise here a few of those questions:

(1) As regards the trial following the murder of Kirov. I had told you how much it would be essential to let the foreign public know the charges against the conspirators. But it was not done. (Here Rolland cited an article by Trotsky in the French journal *Verite* where Trotsky wrote: "The Kirov case has been used for desroying tens of people manifestly devoted to the Revolution but also opposed to the arbitrariness and privileges of the dominant caste.") People are saying that the charges against Zinoviev and Kamenev are absolutely without foundation. And Trotsky is demanding that an international commmission having members with irreproachable credentials be set up who will scrupulously examine the arrests, the trials, the executions and the deportations.Trotsky is severely criticising me and asking me to be a member of this commission knowing full well that I would refuse and this refusal would be the proof of the fear that the friends of the USSR have to throw light on the affair.

(2) I have a letter from an Israeli citizen who fights for the Palestinians and who says that there is anti-Semitism in the USSR where the Jews are repressed when they try to converse in their own language.

(3) Barthelemy de Light —an anti-war individual, well-known internationally—has written a letter where he speaks of atrocities in the USSR against the Dukhobar community which is innocent of any anti-Soviet act and which simply wants to pursue its own religious conviction that includes refusal to accept military service.

(4) I have received letters from the Italian anti-fascists informing me that their anti-fascist comrade Petrini has been handed over to Mussolini's police by the Soviet government

(5) Trotsky's wife is circuating letters, saying that her son Serge, a professor in a Moscow technical school, and his wife

have been arrested. She is affirming that the couple is absolutely innocent, and that the arrest is an act of vengeance against Trotsky. This should be answered by facts.Let me stop here with the list of questions which I have been facing.They demand answers. These are having very bad effects. I am witnessing an increasing number of courageous people desisting from the common action of defending the USSR and who are increasingly joining the various groups who, while combating fascism, are also attacking Soviet policies. A number of newspapers also belong to this tendency. I am sad to see among them a number of my friends who, I know, are sincere revolutionaries.

Dear Comrade

I do not ask you to answer me personally.It is not a question touching me only. I am too old and far too distant from Paris to be able to assume the role of an information centre. But such a centre for diffusing information about the events in the Soviet Union is necessary so that people can be aware of the happenings in the USSR. I have already cited what you had told me, namely, "we do not inform and we do not arm sufficiently our friends. We will try to correct this lacuna."

Yours truly
Romain Rolland
[March 18, 1937]

Dear Comrade Stalin,

Once again I am addressing you, taking the opportunity of your permission you had accorded me when I had spoken to you two years ago.

On the eve of trial of Bukharin and without contesting the charges brought against him, I appeal to your high spirit of humanity and comprehension of the higher interests of the USSR. An inteligence of Bukharin's order is wealth for his country. This can and should be conserved for the benefit of Soviet science and thought in general. If the intelligence has failed due to detestable ideologies, proper punishment must be meted out; still one should save the individual of scientific value misled by these ideologies but who has admitted and regretted his faults and shown readiness to combat them.

One hundred and fifty years ago, the revolutionary tribunal of Paris had condemned to death the genius Lavoisier, the chemist. We in France, the ardent admirers of Robspierre and the committee of public safety, have been suffering from regret and remorse from this execution. Allow me also to invoke a memory which is dear to both of us. I witnessed the deep affectionate friendship which bound these two persons together. In the name of Gorky, I ask you to pardon Bukharin. Whatever his guilt, such a person cannot be compared with those who have preceded him.He can still honour the Soviet thought and be a witness to your spirit of magnanimity.

[Sptember 16, 1937]

Dear Comrade Stalin,

I have earlier written to you regarding the individuals more or less engaged in politics.This time I write to you concerning a dear friend of mine for whom I have great respect—Dr. Oscar Hartoch of the Institute of Experimental Medicine of Leningrad. He was arrested in August this year on the charge of agitation and propaganda. Nothing could be more distant from his character.This is a man solely absorbed by his research, particularly in the field of epidemiology. A modest, shy person, he has always been aloof from all political agitation, and this aloofness has accentuated since the death of his wife, which has overwhelmed him. He has been living with his sister who has come from Switzerland to look after him. I have known them for the last twenty years and am bound with them in fraternal friendship. I fear that Dr. Hartoch's suffering will further increase given his already poor health, and at the same time his absence will cause enormous problems for the number of doctors working under him disorganising their work. Permit me, dear Comrade Stalin, to ask you to intervene, so that the inquiry concerning Dr. Hartoch is not prolonged and thereby he, as I am sure, could be cleared of the charge.

In Context:

(1) Rolland did not get the authorisation to publish the conersation.

(2) Zinoviev and Kamenev, accused of being anti-Soviet and Trotskyst, were condemned to death and executed in 1936. Rehabilitated in 1988.

(3) The language of the Jewish people was not Hebrew but Yiddish in central Europe and Russia.

(4) Nathalie Trotsky, in her circular letter of June 1, 1935, asked for Romain Rolland, Andre Gide, Bernard Shaw and other friends of the Soviet Union to take the initiative in forming a commission of enquiry in agreement with the USSR.

(5) Bukharin was arrested on February 27, 1937. The trial was for "Rightists and anti-Soviet Trotskysts" (March 2 and 3, 1937). Rehabilitated in 1988.

(6)Hartch was arrested on August 2, 1937, freed on May 29, 1938 due to the intervention of Rolland with Stalin. Rearrested in May 1941, as a "German agent", executed on December 25, 1942. Rehabilitated in 1956.

[Source: Foundation Gabriel Peri]

(*Frontier*, December 25-31, 2016)

13

The Tribal Question in India

Ranjit Sau

The world's first flower of democracy bloomed in ancient Greece, in the wake of a military innovation. The manufacture of weapons had advanced considerably. The city-states now had the technology to equip large armies instead of relying on a small squadron of charioteers. They began to deploy heavily armed infantry replacing the old-fashioned warriors who had fought in single combat. Warfare could no longer be the privilege of the nobility. Henceforth anybody who could afford to equip himself with the requisite weapons (*hopla*)—be he lord or farmer—could join this prestigious troop, regardless of rank or birth. With the hoplite army, a new equality was born.

Hoplite fighting was distinguished by the phalanax, a tightly packed body of men, standing shoulder to shoulder, eight deep. Each soldier held his circular shield to protect his left side and gripped the right shoulder of the man next to him. The hoplite army was a people's army; the citizenry had become an army. The hoplite reform transformed Greece and laid the foundations of a deliberately constituted democracy. A farmer who fought next to a nobleman in the phalan would never see the aristocracy in the same way again.

In 510 BC, Sparta attacked Athens. Led by Cleisthenes, son of a tyrant, the Athenians expelled the invaders, and installed him as city magistrate. Within three years, startling reforms were introduced. Cleisthenes abolished the traditional myriad of tribes and reassigned everyone to ten units often, thereby transforming a tribal city into a city state that grew into the strongest military, commercial, artistic and intellectual power along the eastern shore of the Mediterranean Sea. Virtually the same reform would produce even more astonishing results for Mongols on the steppes of inner Asia near two thousand years hence. Members of the people's legislative council were elected annually from the middle classes, and could hold office only twice in their lifetime. As a result most farmers, artisans and merchants would serve on the council at some point, and thus become citizens in an entirely new and meaningful way. This was the most egalitarian polity yet devised, and it had an electrifying effect on the Greek world. That was the first organised form of democracy in the world. Who did it? The reorganised tribals of Athens did it over two-thousand-five-hundred years ago.

The anthropology and history of tribes had been composed largely by appointed scribes at the service of colonists. By their emphasis on the destructive aspects of a tribe's campaign, and their neglect of its contributions to trade, discovery, and the political and cultural institutions of the countries affected, chroniclers produced a picture at once incomplete, lurid and distorted. As a result, the common conception of tribal life even now remains hazy, if not confused, hence polarised—idyllic at one extreme, wretched at the other.

India today faces a radical insurgency commonly known as Maoist (Communist Party of India (Maoist)), or Naxal (after the armed struggle beginning in Naxalbari, West Bengal, 1967) centred at present in the forests that are mostly the home of tribals. So the insurgency is now regarded as virtually a tribal uprising, adding apparently a new chapter in the annals of tribals across the globe, being not a campaign to conquer land or colonise the natives, but an ambitious struggle to capture political power and achieve social and economic justice for all.

In this article the curtain rises with a global scene of the tribes which are among those who have paved the way for modern civilisation. The next scene shows the variety of some contributions made by some tribes in India and some others who are now isolated and branded as 'tribals'. With this comparative perspective, one should look at the current events flowing from the tribes' unrest in India. What to do now, that is the question before the government, the people and the Naxals.

Makers of Civilisation

The most civilised nations of modern Europe issued from the woods of Germany: and in the rude institutions of those barbarians we may still distinguish the original principles of our present laws and manners.

—Edward Gibbon

The term 'tribe' in English derives from Latin *tribus* referring to the original tripartite ethnic division of the Roman state. Many anthropologists use it for societies organised largely on the basis of kinship. Here in India, officially 'a tribe is an administrative and political concept.'[1] What is missing in this approach is the social and economic aspect of tribehood.

To comprehend the nature and variety of tribes, a sample of six has been taken: Three of Europe, viz. Vikings, Goths, and Vandals; two from Asia, viz. Scythians, and Mongols: one from America, viz. the natives of the United States. The first five are the epitome of ingenuity, creative destruction, and domination: the last one is a victim of brute power and exploitation. What makes such differences among them?

Vikings: England was founded by tribes—Germanic and Scandinavian—since the first century AD. This island owes its name to a Germanic tribe the Angles. Explorers, warriors, merchants and pirates the Vikings of Scandinavia, colonised wide areas of Europe between the 8th and 11th centuries. They sailed most of the North Atlantic, reached south of North Africa and East Russia, Constantinople and the Middle East. The Vikings landed in North America and set up a short-lived settlement in Canada. The three centuries of Viking dominance is remembered in history as the Viking Age. Geographically the Viking Age may be assigned not only to Scandinavian lands (modern Denmark, Norway, Sweden) but also the adjacent territories under North Germany.

It was the pressure of history, geography and economics, and their religion and seafaring arts, which made the Vikings distinctive in their day. The population had outgrown the agricultural potential of their Scandinavian homeland. For a coastal people with superlative naval technology, it made sense to expand overseas in the face of the youth bulge effect at home.

Trade between western Europe and the rest of Eurasia suffered as the Roman Empire fell in the 5th century. The rise of Islam in the 7th century had affected trade with western Europe. By opening new routes the Vikings profited in many ways including commerce.[2]

Goths: Barbarians of "the woods of Germany". Goths and Vandals are arguably the senior cousins of Vikings; the three had their roots in Scandinavia. They had worshipped in the town Upsal of Sweden at the same temple of three principal deities: the god of war (Thor), the goddess of fertility and the god of thunder—a religion adapted to the climate and the people. Goths and Vandals are cited by chroniclers more often for their "barbarism" in combat than their contiuation of Roman culture in Late Antiquity and their long-lasting kingdoms in North Africa.

The Goths launched one of the first major invasions of the Roman Empire in 262. By 271 their force was defeated, and some of the survivors were settled within the empire while another part joined the Roman army. The Goth nation would rise again and plunder Asia minor, Greece and Italy.

They sacked Rome in 410, and came to rule most of the Iberian Peninsula, only to yield to the Muslim Umayyad invasion in 711.

Vandals: During the late 5th century, the Vandals entered the late Roman Empire and looted Rome in 455. Although that pillage did not exceed that of the other invaders of ancient times, the modern writers blamed the Vandals for the event. This led to the coinage of 'vandalism', meaning senseless spoiling, especially defacing of artworks.

The Vandal conquest of the North African coast was a strategic move to raid the Mediterranean Sea, much like the

Vikings. They built a fleet to plunder the Mediterranean.

This brief narrative of the three tribes' success in a project affecting other peoples requires certain comparative advantages and superior capability. Three main elements, trade, piracy and raiding were Norse activities long before the Viking Age. The quick-in-quick-out Viking raids could hardly have been possible until the Scandinavian shipwrights had brought the sailing ship to a higher degree of excellence. For the long Atlantic voyages, the first requirement was the mariner's ability to fix his latitude.

The advanced technology of the Vikings gave the sun's midday latitude week by week throughout the year. This or similar information recorded on so simple an object as a marked stick would give the mariner an indication of his then latitude as compared with a known place. Any observation of the midday sun or, if need be, of the Pole Star, even by so crude a method as the measurement of a shadow cast at noon or the calculation of the Star's height above the horizon expressed in terms of one's own arm, hand or thumb was a fair guide of latitude, which on the western voyages were more important than longitude.

Scythians: Horse-riding nomadic pastoral Scythians were an ancient Iranian (Persian) group of tribes who arrived from the Caucasus. Asians knew them as Shaka. India today has two systems of dating, one the familiar Gregorian calendar of BC/AD and the other based on the Shaka era which is reckoned to have begun in India in 78 AD. Shakas receive numerous mentions in Indian texts including the epics Ramayana and Mahabharata.

The Shakas segmented into a variety of junior kingdoms, i.e. satrapies, readily assimilated to Indian society and made a lasting impression. Rudradaman the Shaka king in north-west India, staunchly upheld *dharma*, possibly in imitation of Ashoka, with whose edicts he happily shared the rock space. It was this Shaka king who ushered in an unprecedented and great comeback of classical Sanskrit as it was by his memorial being inscribed in classical Sanskrit rather than the conventional forms of Prakrit, Magadhi or Pali. Arguably, the Satrap's use of

Sanskrit was a method followed to endear a ruler of foreign descent to the indigenous ruling class 'to mitigate the lamentable choice of parents on the part of the Satrap (a Shaka king)'. To be sure, the Sanskrit inscription soon became accepted by the rulers of Sumatra, Java, Indo-China and other parts of Indianised Southeast Asia. The employment of a prestige language lent distinction and authority even to the non-Indic dynasties.[3]

Mongols: Nurtured in the harsh winds of the barren steppe, Genghis Khan built the Mongol Empire in the early 13th century. Unaware of the ancient Greek history, in the wilderness of Mongolia he had virtually replicated the model of tribal reform as of the classical Athens under Cleisthenes, cited above.

His army subjugated more lands and people in 25 years than the Romans did in four hundred. In nearly every country the Mongols conquered, they brought an unprecedented rise in cultural communication, expanded trade, and a blossoming of civilisation. Vastly more progressive than his European and Asian counterparts, Genghis Khan abolished torture, granted universal religious freedom and smashed feudal systems of aristocratic privilege. Grown up in a world of excessive tribal violence in Mongolia, he left behind the epic story of how the modern civilisation was made.[4]

Native Americans in the US: In the 1995 US Census the indigenous tribes expressed preference to be known as Indians or American Indians, rather than the assumed particular name, Native Americans. To them India is not a tribute from the country of India but derived from the Spanish expression *En Dio*, meaning "In God." The first colonist who entered the US in 1513 was a Spanish explorer.

In 1924 the natives were granted US citizenship. In 1975 they were given the power of self-determination. Now there are 562 federally recognised tribal governments within the country. These tribes possess the right to, among others, form their own governments to enforce laws (both civil and criminal), to tax, to license and regulate activities, to zone and to exclude persons from tribal territories. Limitations of tribal powers of self-government include the same limitations applicable to states; for example, neither tribes nor states have the power to make war, engage in foreign relations, or issue coins (this includes paper currency).

The pace of assimilation of tribes in the general society has been slow. In the 18th century, George Washington observed that the natives were equal but their society was inferior. He encouraged the civilising process with a view to assimilate them to the general society. In the next century, boarding schools were established for the children. But the experience often proved traumatic to the students who were forbidden to speak their native language, taught Christianity and denied the right to practise their native religions and in numerous other ways forced to abandon their native identities and adopt European-American culture.

Far from forming a single ethnic group, the Native Americans are divided into several hundred ethnic-linguistic groups. Gambling has become a leading profession. Although many tribes have casinos the impact is widely debated. Some tribes feel that casinos and their proceeds destroy culture from the inside out.

The economic status of the native Americans is grim. They rank at the bottom of nearly every statistics: highest teen suicide rate of all minorities, highest rate of teen pregnancy, highest high school dropout, lowest per capita income and unemployment rates between 50% and 90%. A classic report of the Harvard Project mentioned the barriers to economic development of the tribes. An incomplete list is as follows: lack of access to capital, poor natural resources in their territories, disadvantages due to the distance of markets and the high cost of transportation. And tribal culture gets on the way. "A general lack of education and experience about business is a significant challenge to prospective entrepreneurs."[5]

The six sets of tribes narrated in this section display diverse propensities and varying degrees of success in their endeavours. One thing, though, is common: the real unbiased history of the tribes have not yet been written in full. Among all these sets, we shall see presently, the last one bears a good deal of conformity with the one that is going to be analysed. The American Indian tribes and the South Asian Indian tribes would look much like cousins in the book of history. Both were forced to serve as slaves, and both are not yet assimilated in their respective general societies.

A Model of Analysis

The entire course of Indian history shows tribal elements being fused into the general society. —D.D. Kosambi

The pastoral Vedic age yielded to the agrarian era. The first major village settlement was promoted under state control. Chanakya, also known as Kautilya, the prime minister in the imperial court of Chandragupta Maurya in the late 4th century BC described in his treatise *Arthasastra* the procedure of mobilising the tribes to be herded into crown villages to toil on farmland as virtual slaves. "Agent provocateurs should gain access to all the tribes, discover the possible sources of jealousy, hatred, contention, among them; should disseminate the seeds of progressive dissension. Let those of higher rank, within the tribe, be discouraged from eating at a common table with, and marriage with, those of lower standing. Tribesmen with lower rank should, on the other hand, be instigated to insist upon commensality and intermarriage with the lower. The lesser should be provoked to claim equality of status in family and prowess. Public decisions and tribal customs should be brought to dissolution by insisting upon the contrary." This episode of inhuman exploitation of tribes in ancient India resembles the fate of their American counterparts, more than two millenia later. In the 19th century, the incessant westward expansion of the United States incrementally compelled large numbers of Native Americans to resettle further west, often by force, almost always reluctantly. By the pressure of the Indian Removal Act of 1830, as many as 100,000 relocated to the West, resulting in the deaths of thousands.

The next step in India would ossify the caste system and make the tribals destitute ever since. A brief history of the lowly strata of society, viz. Scheduled castes, and outcasts of the society, i.e. tribals, is as follows.

Peace and trade during the Gupta period (AD 300-500) had stimulated village settlements by private enterprise; rural economy thrived. Meanwhile, the urban nouveau riche, so fond of Mediterranean coral, exotic wines and slaves for household service, concubines and entertainment, the art and craftsmanship of the Roman-Greek world, exhausted the country's foreign exchange reserves. A critical shortage of coin-money for domestic business transactions was inevitable. To solve the currency problem the crown took an ingenious step of assigning caste-based artisans to every village such that barter exchange within the village would do. Each village was allowed its precisely required number of blacksmiths, carpenters, potters and other artisans, not exceeding 12 in total. Each artisan was entitled to a certain portion of harvest from the peasants. Every village thus became self-sufficient, cash-free and disconnected from other villages and the rest of the world. As a result, the caste system was sealed firmly across the villages. The economy became stagnant under the rigid caste rules, being incapable of absorbing additional hands. Unemployment mounted. Caste groups prevented the mastery of finer techniques. Very few could, because of caste, skin cattle, tan hides, or work in leather, all low occupations. Some tribesmen might become basket-makers, without learning how to weave cloth or spin yarn. On the other hand, given the social structure, not every village could support a whole guild of blacksmiths, leather-workers, or bark-weavers. The jobless unfortunates headed towards the wilderness of forests or hills and turned into wretched tribes ever since. History moves at three levels: (a) the one which is almost changeless, the history of man in relation to his natural surroundings; (b) the second, a movement of gentle rhythms, of groups and groupings, which is the traditional social history; and (c) the third, the history of not so much of man in general as of man in particular. In other words, history is shaped by the forces of nature, the structure of society and the role of individuals. This formulation is a contribution by French thinkers, who consider it as a model of the Total History. Comparative reference among tribes can be better organised in the framework of Total History.[6] For example, the pathos of the tribals of India and those of the US had certain similarities in part because the social orders in these two countries had been arguably comparable in terms of the exercise of authority by the rulers. If the European colonists imposed their religion upon the American natives, the royal authority of the Maurya Empire in India had done about the same on the tribes in the labour camps of India.

Development and Progress

Whatever we understand and enjoy in human products instantly becomes ours, wherever they might have their origin. Let me feel with unalloyed gladness that all the great glories of man are mine.

—Rabindranath Tagore

The tribal insurgence inspired by the Naxals and Maoists is officially marked as the most serious internal threat to the security of India. The rebels have declared their battle against the incumbent political regime.

But what would we replace it with; what would be their social, economic, political stance? All this is kept obscure, unknown to the people at large. An armed campaign that rests on mere negative ground, and is reticent about its positive aspects, if any, does not bode public credibility. Power might flow from the barrel of guns, but it would find itself exhausted in no time once bullets fall short. Man does not live on politics alone.

To tame the adversaries, pundits and the government both offer a two-prong strategy: *Panchayat Raj* and *Development,* in the *jangal mahal,* the forest habitat of tribals. To begin with, 'the historic, revolutionary pro-tribal legislation', the Panchayat (Extension of Scheduled Areas) Act (PESA) was intended to bring a fresh air of democracy nourished with the active participation and enthusiasm. Far away from the centre of power and civilisation, the thatched huts of the aborigines in *jangals* would flicker in dim light.

But the record of Native Americans does not corroborate. They were granted even the power of Self-Determination, together on the rights on par with those that are enjoyed by federal states such as New York and California. Despite the enormous political mandates, the tribes languished in remote isolated, introvert localities: bereft of markets, schools, colleges, universities and above all, the scope of belonging to the universal civilisation.

What is meant by development in this context? In the lists of government projects, development is measured by: construction of roads, digging tube-wells, building schools, hospitals and the like—all these materials informed by a page of the 'materialistic interpretation of history', the one that leaves out the individual human beings which is the third element in the design of the Total History.

The fifteenth-century Renaissance in Europe was the epoch of the individual; "the development of a universal capacity to think of yourself, in a fundamental way, as an individual." distinct from being the member of a family, group, clan or tribe. An individual was now viewed as a repository of all that human beings had achieved, 'a point of unity for all that had been thought and done by man, within the mind restored to consciousness of its own sovereign faculty.' This was a static concept of the nature of man, harking back to the past, accumulating heirlooms. By the 19th century, a dynamic conception of man emerged: 'man figured not as an essential starting point but as a destination, less given to a set of intrinsic qualities than the goal of an epochal and never-to-be completed process.' If there is a 'human condition', it is the condition of being always uncomsummated. Man is not a simply unchanging entity at all but a sign of change, a site of continuous transformation. The process of man's progress is endless. An 'individual' is a carrier of that eternal movement, a site of great continuous becoming, a person worthy of dignity and respect.[7]

Every individual, not excluding the tribal one, deserves full opportunities to realise the potentialities he desires, to be a part of the general society of the country, and to have access to the universal civilisation. This kind of 'progress' of the individual would be conceivable if tribes are not confined in the so-called 'scheduled areas', and lulled by the bait of more *aranyer adhikar,* the rights to forest resources.

Help every tribal child to bcome a poet, doctor, engineer, musician, postman, football player, or accountant, or a master of another profession of his or her choice. In this respect, the fifth schedule of the Constitution of India seems restrictive to the possibilities of tribals. The tribes of India are fragmented, scattered, overburdened with innumerable dialects, lack of dialogue among themselves, and unfamiliar with the outside world. Don't keep them blind, tied in the darkness of the proverbial, primitive 'cave' of Plato.

REFERENCES

1. Anthropological Survey of India, 1994: *The Scheduled Tribes,* xiii.
2. Gwyn Jones, 1984: *A History of Vikings.*
3. John Keay, 2000: *India: A History.*
4. Jack Weatherlord, 2004: *Genghis Khan and the Making of the Modern World.*
5. The Harvard Project of American Indian Economic Development, 2008: *The State of the Native Nations: Conditions Under US Policies of Self-Determination.*
6. Fernand Braudel, 1980: *On History.*
7. Ranjit Sau, 2009: *The Foundation of Democracy in India,* May 30-June 5, 2010.

14

Identity Politics: The Crisis of Identity

Santosh Rana

India is a vast country with a population of about 1,100 millions. If a person is selected at random from this sea of people, he/she would be found to have a number of identities. One identity is based on his specific mother-tongue, which may be Hindi, Bengali, Santali, Telugu, Assamese or any other language. Again, the religious community to which he/she belongs may mark him/her out as a Hindu, or a Muslim, or a Christian, or a Buddhist, or a worshipper of nature like the adivasis. Besides, he/she has his/her caste/identity. Caste divisions are recognised only in Hinduism, but a glance at the Indian society would reveal that even the followers of Christianity or Islam have become stratified into castes. Over and above these considerations, every person is either a male or a female(barring a very small group of bisexuals), and that too constitutes an aspect of his/her identity. Finally, whatever the linguistic, religious, caste or gender identity of the person, he/she participates in the social process of social production and gets a share of social product in a specific manner. He/she may be an agricultural labourer, a brick-kiln worker, a sharecropper, a small owner cultivator or a factory or plantation worker. Alternatively, he/she may be a rural rich farmer or non-cultivating landowner, the owner of a factory or tea garden. Again, he/she may be a government employee, teacher of a school or college, employee of a bank or insurance company or something else. In the Census records of India, these diverse identities of every person are put on record. This enables us to know the number of males and females, and the number of persons engaged in each broad occupational category.

But after independence, the practice of recording the caste and ethnic identities of the people was stopped, except for scheduled castes and adivasis. On the eve of the census of 2001, a strong demand was raised for recording the caste identities of persons, but the then ruling NDA government refused to accept it. This year, the same demand has been raised and the Government of India has accepted it. It is noticeable that the political parties that took the lead in this regard were from the NDA as well as the UPA, while the leftists, although not as vocal as them, did not offer any opposition. The Census operations undertaken before 1951, the last being that of 1931, noted the caste identities of people. At the time of the first Census of independent India, the Central Government led by Nehru decided to stop the practice of recording caste identities. Now the descendants belonging to the third next generation of successors are compelled to reintroduce this practice.

An analogy can be found from the story of the changing attitude of the Central Government towards the Other Backward Classes. When in 1953, the Kaka Kalelkar Commission, appointed by the Government of India, recommended reservation for these classes according to population in respect of education and jobs, this was turned down by the government. In 1978, the Government of India appointed the Second Backward Class Commission and after a long period of haggling, implementation of its recommendations began as late as 1990. In today's India, neither the Congress nor any other political party is in a position to oppose reservation for the OBCs. But the most significant change has taken place in West Bengal. When in 1978, the Mandal Commission came to West Bengal and sought the opinion of the State Government, the latter formed a one-man committee, the lone member being Mr. Binay Chaudhuri. The committee, within one month, produced its report denying the existence of Other Backward Classes in West Bengal. This opinion of the Government of West Bengal is recorded in writing in the report of the Mandal Commission. When, after a great deal of turmoil in national politics, 27% of reservation for the OBCs in education and jobs was introduced nationally, the Government of West Bengal refused to implement it. After much haggling, 7% reservation was introduced in West Bengal, but that too in jobs, not in education. In the 1980s, any talk of reservation for Muslims in government jobs in West Bengal evoked only furious opposition from the leftists. Now, after the defeat in the Lok Sabha polls of 2009 and the civic polls of 2010, the Left Front Government has reckoned Muslims as OBCs and has accordingly announced 10% reservation for them. Besides, it has amended the Panchayet Act in order to provide reservation for the OBCs in the panchayats, something that no other Indian state has done. The position of the Left Front Government is thus entirely different from that of the 1980s. But the fact remains that the structure of the Bengali society has remained more or less the same as it was in 1977, and hence there were no other backward classes in West Bengal in 1977. There is no reason why such classes should come to exist later.

It is easily comprehensible that these changes of declaration and practice are motivated by considerations of votes. The Congress Government ruling in Delhi too is modifying its policies for the same purpose. In a democratic polity, this is not an offence. But these changes contain an implicit recognition that the electorate, while exercising their franchise, are mindful about their respective identities, which means that they are taking into account the possible gains and losses of their respective identities. They are asking questions on various issues; for example, on the entry of Muslims into government jobs, the opening of the doors of higher education and jobs for OBCs, the right of the adivasis of the Jharkhand cultural region (*jangal mahal*) and the Kamtapuris to be instructed in their mother tongue, and so on and so forth. Yet it is not that these issues were raised always during election campaigns. During the Lok Sabha polls of 1977, the main question was whether the Emergency should continue or the democratic rights of the people should be restored. The assembly polls of that year in West Bengal brought to the fore not only the issue of ending the misrule and authoritarianism of the Congress, but that of meeting the demand of the rural toiling masses on the issues of wages, barga-recording, declaration and distribution of surplus land, etc. In the subsequent elections of West Bengal too the common demands of agricultural labourers and poor peasants played a significant role. Considering the country as a whole, it can be observed that just as the Congress held official power at the centre till 1977, it generally reigned in the states as well. During those years, the question of identity did not play any important role in the states except Tamil Nadu. For example, when the Nehru Government refused to accept the recommendations of the Kaka Kalelkar Commission, there was no nationwide movement and the monopoly of the Congress in ministry making remained unimpaired. In order to understand the significance of these experiences, we shall try to find the connections among the multifaceted identity of a person of Indian society, his/her social standing and his/her economic gain.

Identity and Achievement

After the use of iron in productive activities was introduced, vast tracts of the Doab region lying between the Ganga and the Yamuna were brought under settled cultivation and agriculture began to yield surplus on a sizeable scale. The concentration and reinvestment of this surplus, i.e. bringing new areas under settled cultivation and concomitant growth of industry and commerce, required a strong state, which the Mauryas created. The state owned land, mines and other instruments of production. The kings, priests, ministers, army commanders and departmental royal officials used to supervise the various departments of administration and production, and used to receive salaries from the state. Agricultural labourers working on state farms and craftsmen producing under state supervision were also salaried workers. The difference between the salaries of direct producers and those of royal officials was enormous.

The ratio between the salary of a minister or an army commander and that of an agricultural labourer was 500:1 or 1000:1. Thus a state class appropriated and consumed the surplus. The process of social stratification on the basis of caste had already begun and the state class was composed of the *dwija* castes. On the other hand,workers and peasants belonged to the lower castes, having no right to education and official employment. Alongside state ownership of land, the system of private ownership had also come into existence, but these owners were upper caste people. Later a complex caste system came to be the basis of social stratification, and in this pyramid like structure, the extent of the share of the social product to be received by a caste was determined basically by its relative position in this ladder. Even before the growth of capitalist relations, class divisions began to appear among castes, sometimes giving rise to the break-up of one specific caste into several castes. After the rise and growth of capitalist forms and relations, such class divisions were accentuated, and particularly from among the intermediate castes grew (e.g. the, Sadgops, Telis and Mahisyas in Bengal, the Khandayets in Orissa, the Yadavs and Kurmis in Bihar, the Yadavs and Jats in North India) a class of landowners and rich farmers, and one section of them began to invest surplus in trade and commerce. After the abolition of the system of zamindari, one segment of these intermediate castes, which had been used to pay rents to landlords, became ryots. But they were backward in respect of education, jobs and share of political power. The ruling structure that began to function after independence made it incumbent for individuals and groups to use the political ladder for upward mobility.

In Indian society, one index of the privilege or deprivation of a person is his/her caste status. But that is not the only index. Another index is language. In colonial India, all Indian languages had equal dignity or indignity. After independence, Hindi is the only Indian official language. The other official language is English. Among all the linguistic groups of India, there is a tiny section to which English is synonymous with the mother tongue. These people have no problem with our system of official languages. But among the broad majority of Indians, the Hindi-speaking section enjoys a privileged position compared with others. Again, there are some linguistic groups whose languages have no official recognition even at the state level. For example, Santali, notwithstanding its inclusion in the Eighth Schedule of the Indian Constitution, has as yet been recognised as an official language in any state of India. Kamtapuri of North Bengal has no kind of recognition whatsoever. The number of Santali-speaking people in India is about seven million. This number may appear small in the Indian context, but there are many countries with a population that is even less. Similarly, the number of Kamtapuri-speaking people living in West Bengal, Assam and Bihar is not less than five million. There is a standing demand for a separate Kamtapur state, and there is a political movement on this basis. The area of North Bengal where Kamtapuris live has among its population Bengalis, Gorkhas and Jharkhandis too. Hence to grant a territorial autonomy for Kamtapuris only is deeply problematic. But there should be no difficulty in granting official recognition to the Kamtapuri language.

On the all-India plane, it is observable that the southern states are always vocal against the status of Hindi as the sole official language. Mainly on their demand, English has been retained as the official language alongside Hindi. But this is not a real solution. There are some complexities in the process of granting equal status (official status) to languages like Tamil, Telugu, Bengali, Gujarati, Hindi and other Indian languages, but these complexities are not insurmountable. Rather equal status for the languages is the sine qua non for the preservation of the unity of a vast multi-lingual country like India.

Outside caste, nationality and language there is another identity in the Indian society, that of religion. As many as 80% of the people of India are Hindus. But there is something problematic in this estimate. In the Census operations there are many that are recorded, as Hindus but do not follow anything ordained by the Hindu customs. For example, all the non-

Christian adivasis are reckoned as Hindus, although a large section of the adivasis do not rely on Brahmin priests for performing the prayers in ceremonies like worship, funerary rites, marriages, etc. Again, there are some communities whose Hinduisation is only partial. The Kurmis and Mahatos of the Jharkhand cultural region are such communities, and there is a strong clamour among them for the scheduled caste status. Again, sizeable sections of the Jharkhandi adivasi population, e.g. the Santals, Mundas, Oraons, Mahalis, Malpahariyas, etc, live in Assam. They have scheduled tribe status everywhere in the country except Assam. This problem exists elsewhere as well. Hence it is a legitimate conjecture that although the Census figures show the adivasis to be 7.5% of the population, in reality this percentage is higher. Our surmise is that it is more than 10%. Among these adivasis there are political movements for the recognition of language, various kinds of autonomy including a separate state, recognition as a separate linguistic community, etc.

Again, the socio-economic conditions of all the scheduled castes are not the same. In almost every state, there are one or two scheduled castes that are far advanced in relation to others owing to various historical reasons, and it is they who appropriate the reservation facilities in education and jobs. The namasudra community of West Bengal is such an advanced caste group. The Chamars of Uttar Pradesh and the Malas of Andhra Pradesh are such groups. For this reason, movements for separate quotas by relatively backward scheduled castes are seen.

Conditions of Muslims in India: Muslims constitute the second largest religious community in India. There is a small section among them whose forefathers came from Turkey, Afghanistan, Iran or Arab lands. But the vast majority of them were low-caste people who were converted to Islam. The caste system of India is so strong that even after apostasy, the caste identities of these people were not obliterated. Islam does not recognise caste distinctions, but Indian Muslims are divided into castes. Although this division is not as rigid as that of the

Hindu society, Muslims take into account caste identity before entering into matrimonial alliances.

The Constitution of the Indian State is secular in the sense that it has not formally conferred any special privilege to any particular religious community or has deprived any community. But the reality is different. For various historical reasons (e.g. self-imposed distance of Muslims from English education till 1857, the lower-caste origin of a large section of Muslims, etc) the participation of Muslims in higher education and jobs was low even during partition. After partition a section of affluent middle class Muslims migrated to Pakistan and the share of Muslims in higher education and jobs suffered a further decline. For example, Muslims had 17% of government jobs in West Bengal in 1947, which came down to 7% at the time of the end of Congress rule in 1977, and by 2007, at the time of the publication of the Sachar Report, it fell to as low as to 2%. Yet Muslims constitute about 25% of the total population of West Bengal. It should be mentioned that a government job in India is not just one kind of employment, and with it are attached some social prestige and various economic powers. In case of bank loans and various social services too (schools, drinking water, health centres, ICDS scheme, etc) Muslims are in a state of deprivation. Although the extent of this deprivation has inter-state variations, its existence is an all-India reality. To add to it, there is coercion by the state and non-state agencies. In the eyes of the state, every Muslim is an offender or potential offender. It is stated in the report of the Sachar Committee, "Our analysis shows that although there are inter-state variations in the conditions of Muslims, this community is lagging behind in all states in respect of all the yardsticks of development. The actual reality is that the conditions of Muslims are slightly better than scheduled castes/tribes, but much below those of the Hindu OBCs, other minorities or general Hindus, the majority of whom are upper castes). Among the states in which Muslims live in large numbers, the conditions of this community in West Bengal, Bihar, Uttar Pradesh and Assam are indeed very poor. Besides this deficient development,the problem has been aggravated by the fact that there is a strong notion among Muslims that they are being deprived or kept outside the process of development."

If the notion that Muslims are in a state of deprivation is an all-pervasive one among them, it is only natural that they would like to use the polls in such a manner that would end this deprivation and suppression, or at least lessen its intensity.

Identity-Based Political Parties and Movements: Of the identity-based movements that have taken place in India, the oldest is the Dravid movement of Tamil Nadu. In terms of sustainability too, this movement was a long one, although it underwent many divisions and changes later. Periyar Ramaswami Naikar—he later renounced the title Naikar—may be called the founder and architect of the movement. In Periyar's thoughts, there was an intermingling of Tamil nationalism and anti-Brahminism; the question of women's emancipation too was an important aspect of his movement. His 'self-respect movement' combined these elements. He toured Russia and was deeply influenced by the system of work for everybody, education and health for all, and particularly freedom for women. The Dravid movement came to exercise a powerful influence on the social life of Tamil Nadu. In respect of reduction of infant mortality, enrolment of children in schools, management of ICDS schemes, male-female ratio and many other indicators of social progress, Tamil Nadu ranks among the most advanced states of India. It is the only state in India that, in order to implement 67% reservation for the OBCs, has compelled the Indian state to amend the constitution and has thus defied the obstacle posed by the judgment of Balaji vs State of Mysore case. In the political sphere too, Tamil Nadu has repeatedly played a positive role in providing support to the Anandpur Sahib Resolution as well as various other proposals in favour of a federal structure. In this state, as much as 95% of Muslims have been identified as OBCs and have come within the purview of reservation. The all-India political parties, namely the Congress and the BJP have been reduced to a marginal position in Tamil Nadu, and they cannot do anything there without entering into alliances with some or other Dravid party as subordinate partners.

The movement of the depressed classes, subsequently known as the Dalit movement, led by Dr. B.R. Ambedkar had less local success than that of the Dravid movement. Even Dr. Ambedkar himself could not be elected to the Constituent Assembly from Maharashtra, and had to go there as a representative from Bengal. But in respect of nationwide significance, his thoughts had much greater influence. His Republican Party of India is now divided into many groups, and in Maharashtra, these groups now survive as appendages of the Congress or the BJP. But this upshot has by no means ended the Ambedkarite movement in India; rather it has re-emerged in new places in new forms. The demand for equal dignity for those communities who have over the ages been deprived of the right to property, the right to education and political rights, and on whose blood and sweat the edifice of Indian civilisation has been built, is the demand of revolutionary democracy in the Indian context. Ambedkar came to be the symbol of this revolutionary change. Ambedkar's thoughts grew in contradistinction to those of Gandhi, and through conflicts with the latter.

Gandhi was against untouchability, but was in favour of the caste system. His opinion was that the untouchables should acquire education but should not use it as their means of livelihood. It was his belief that the principle of hereditary occupation was eternal, and if India gave it up, a serious disorder would follow. On the other hand, Ambedkar's slogan was annihilation of caste, the first step towards which was the abolition of the principle of hereditary profession. It is true that Ambedkar's approach had its limitations. In Indian society, the caste system was at the same time the cause and effect of concentration of ownership of land in the hands of upper castes. It was not possible to annihilate the caste system without a revolutionary programme of radical land reform. The subject has appeared theoretically in some of Ambedkar's writings, but his programme did not incorporate land movements. One reason was that Ambedkar laid excessive stress on legal constitutional means for bringing about social change. In a word, he sought emancipation of Dalits within the framework of bourgeois democracy.

Mayawati is the most successful leader of Dalit movements in India so far. She has come to power in a state as large as Uttar Pradesh in a specific historical situation. The emergence of this historical situation can be traced back to 1977, before which the Congress had a monopoly of power in the Centre as well as in most of the states. It was not that there was no deprivation practised on Dalits, adivasis, OBCs, Muslims or various marginal communities, nor that they had no grievances. But the Congress had emerged as the leader of the national movement, and the vocal, advanced sections of all identities had been accommodated within what was known as the Congress system. At the time of the split in the Congress in 1969, Indira Gandhi gave extra importance to the leaders of the lower castes, OBCs, adivasis and Muslims, and although without a majority in the Congress Working Committee, she could establish the section led by her as the real Congress. But the economic policy followed since 1947 was in a crisis, the disaster it had brought to the lives of the people gave birth to countrywide mass protest movements in 1966-67. By 1974, the crisis deepened, and it became necessary to suppress the people by unleashing a phase of repression (*anushasan parva*). Along with it, the contradiction between different imperialist powers became enmeshed with the contradictions among the ruling classes, and in this complicated situation, the internal emergency was imposed. The emergency brought on attacks on all sect ions of people of the country, but the attack was most severe on those identities that were lowly placed in social and economic positions. Dalits, adivasis, OBCs and Muslims were attacked. The consequence was that although the leadership of these identities was with the Congress, the connections of that leadership with the masses were weakened, and in some cases altogether snapped. This was the breakdown of the Congress system. In the Lok Sabha polls of 1977, the main issue was the restoration of democracy, and there was no identity-based demand. But it was that very election that witnessed the rise of identities. From Bihar and the entire North India including Uttar Pradesh, many candidates belonging to the lower castes and OBCs were elected with the ticket of the Janata Party. It was through the Jayaprakash-led movement and the Lok Sabha polls of 1977 that politicians like Lalu Prasad Yadav, Nitish Kumar, Rambila Paswan, Mulayam Singh Yadav, Sharad Yadav, etc came to the fore.

Uttar Pradesh is the largest province of India. Here, after the breakdown of the Congress system, there was no longer any force that was capable of bringing Dalits, OBCs, Muslims and upper castes under a single roof. Again, none of these groups was able to acquire a majority in the polls on its own. Muslims of Uttar Pradesh did not form a party of their own, and they usually exercise their franchise in favour of the non-BJP party that is stronger at the centre. It is more worthwhile to call it a defensive attitude rather than an effort to assert their identity. These circumstances led to a fluid situation in that province, and the BJP, although it won once(on that occasion, the BJP, by raising communal slogans, could acquire many OBC votes), failed to retain the victory. It was followed by various types of coalition governments, such as the BJP-Mayawati coalition and the Mulayam-Mayawati coalition. This period was used by Mayawati to raise the slogan of Dalit rule and thus to consolidate Dalit votes. In the Dalit-dominated areas, some Mulim votes too came over to her side. Thereafter, she replaced the slogan of 'bahujan' (many communities) with 'sarbajan' (all communities) and was able to win a section of upper caste votes. In the last election, however, she got only 32% of total votes polled, but the existence of various alliances and divisions enabled her to form a stable government. Her government has not taken any measure of basic importance (such as land reform) to improve the lot of Dalits, although it has done some work like allotting homestead lands to the homeless or building residential quarters for Dalits under the Indira Abas Yojana. But the scale of such activities are not of such an order that are significantly different from the work done in other states. On the other hand, although the common people are aggrieved at her outrageous exhibition of money, wealth, ornaments and power, Dalits are as yet prone to view it as an 'exhibition of Dalit power.' Until there is a broad-based mass movement in Uttar Pradesh on the basis of radical land reform and other democratic demands, Mayawati will continue to represent a political force.

The Jharkhand movement is very old. Once the Jharkhand party led by Jaipal Singh occupied the place of the principal opposition party in Bihar. But after his joining the Congress, the movement received a setback, to be revived again after Naxalbari. In the 1970s, the Jharkhand Mukti Morcha came into existence and grew through land and anti-usury struggles. Besides, the joint leadership of Binod Mahato and Sibu Soren forged a unity between adivasis and semi-adivasi communities like the Kurmis and Mahatos. In the 1980s, the participation of the CPI(M-L) and other revolutionary forces strengthened the Jharkhand movement, and a possibility emerged of basic democratisation, including the formation of a separate state, of the movement. The Indian ruling classes, apprehensive of such a possibility, purchased one section of the leadership of the movement with the lure of power and pelf. The consequence was a breakdown of the Jharkhand Coordination Committee and a division in the movement, leading to a separation between Binod Mahato and Sibu Soren. Besides, the Jharkhand Mukti Morcha could not settle the question as to the rights of the semi-adivasi communities, reckoned as scheduled tribes till 1935, after the formation of the separate state. Sibu Soren, by embarking on a race for personal and family power, turned himself into a laughing stock.

But the voice against the plunder of the riches of the Jharkhand region by imperialist and corporate capital, raised during the movement, has not been smothered. When Arjun Munda of the BJP was the Chief Minister, he signed MOUs for handing over about 2 lakh hectares of land to the Tatas, Jindals,

Bhusans and other large companies. But nowhere have the companies been able to take possession of land in the face of the pressure of resistance movements.

Neoliberalism and Identity Politics: The neoliberal regime that has come into being in India after 1990 has freed foreign capital from the obligation to secure permission from the central government for investment in a state. A clearance from the central government is necessary for setting up a Special Economic Zone, and for any other industry, a clearance from the forest and environment departments is necessary. Past experience has shown that if the concerned state government agrees, the companies succeed in obtaining clearances by lobbying and bribery in Delhi. In this new situation, all the state governments without exception compete with each other to welcome domestic and foreign big capital. The larger the amount of capital pouring into a state, the greater is the opportunity for plunder. A Chief Minister of Jharkhand, having no party affiliation, took advantage of the volatile political situation of Jharkhand and amassed a few thousand crores of rupees within a span of two years only by selling out mines. In Chhattisgarh, minerals worth quite a few crores of rupees are 'sold' at a price of one lakh rupees. Now illegal mining and attendant corruption are rampant over a vast region including Andhra Pradesh, Maharashtra, Karnataka, Orissa and Jharkhand, and these activities fetch thousands of crores to the companies and corrupt politicians.

Identity-based parties (the DMK in Tamil Nadu, the Mukti Morcha in Jharkhand, Lalu Yadav and Nitish Kumar in Bihar, Mayawati and Mulayam in Uttar Pradesh) have adapted themselves to this plunder of the neoliberal regime. In West Bengal, the Trinamul Congress, although not an identity-based party, is a regional outfit. The same is true of the Biju Janata Dal of Orissa. The Trinamul Congress garnered strength by capitalising on the grievances of the people against neoliberal plunder. But immediately after ascent to power at the Centre, they have declared the policy of banning workers' right to strike and activities of other political parties. They are trying to impress upon the bourgeoisie that they are much more reliable for executing the neoliberal programme.

But under this neoliberal regime, workers, peasants and other toiling people of the country are now faced with large-scale attacks. The problem of suppressed identities is most acute. As the leadership of identity politics has come to support the neoliberal policies, a search for alternatives has begun. A vacuum similar to one that was created after the breakdown of the Congress system is coming into existence. This is a favourable situation for a revolutionary transformation of Indian society. This vacuum can be filled only by a leftist force or a leftist coalition that will stand up against neoliberal policies, will combine the identity-based demands with the basic demands for radical land reform and work, food, education and health for all, and will present a political programme for the broadening of democracy through local power (for example, power in the hands of panchayats or gram samsads) over land, forests, water and mineral resources. Various regions of the country are now witnessing the rise and growth of such leftist forces, although their realisation of the question of broadening of democracy is still incomplete. It may be expected that they will learn through experience and play their necessary role in the revolutionary transformation of Indian society.

(Autumn Number, 2010)

15

Colonel Abu Taher's Uprising

Peter Custers

It has been 35 years since Bangladesh's revolutionary leader Colonel Abu Taher died a martyr's death. Eight and a half months after leading a soldier's insurrection which had spread like wildfire from Dhaka's cantonments to cantonments different districts of Bangladesh, Abu Taher, on July 21, was hanged in Dhaka central jail. The uprising had been short-lived since on the very day when the soldiers started rebelling, November 7, Bangladesh's bourgeoisie regained the initiative. Yet for two full weeks, as both army generals tried to restore 'order' and as Taher's forces tried to regroup, bourgeois rule had come to a virtual standstill. In the end Taher, his close associates and thousands of activists of the party that had backed the rising, the Jatiya Samajtantrik Dal (JSD) were arrested and thrown into jail. He was tried before a secret military tribunal staged inside the Dhaka jail, and was given capital punishment. The execution by hanging was a cowardly act by the military regime that was led by his former friend Ziaur Rahman. It is quite appropriate to evaluate Colonel Taher's legacy by quoting Lenin on the Easter rising against British colonial rule over Ireland. This rising, like Bangladesh's 1975 soldier's insurrection, was a 'failed' uprising, it was crushed before it could gather full strength. Nevertheless, Lenin deeply respected the Irish fighters who had attempted to stage a revolution some one and a half years before the Bolshevik Revolution took place. As he argued: "Whoever expects a 'pure' social revolution will never live to see it. The misfortune of the Irish was that they rose prematurely, when the European revolt of the proletariat had not yet matured. Here there was a 'great popular' revolt which undoubtedly had historical significance." The insurrection carried ideas and ideals which were and are unique. They stand out, compared with the ideas on military strategy and on social transformation which at the time were defended by other currents of the Bangladesh Left.

Moreover, these ideas continue to carry great weight for the contemporary struggle of the oppressed male and female peasants and workers of Bangladesh.

A Brief Witness Account

This evaluation of the soldiers' insurrection is partly based on personal experience. I therefore first wish to recount some of my direct impressions of the November 7th events. On that historic day of November 7, 1975, I happened to wake up early and went for a morning walk from my Elephant Road residence, located close to the beginning of Mirpur Road. This was at 6 o'clock in the morning and as I moved along the main road, I saw a whole series of trucks coming down from the cantonment area's direction, packed with soldiers firing gunshots of joy in the air. It was immediately obvious that the cantonment's soldiers that night had massively responded to a call for insurrection, and that, at this very moment, the attempt to stage a revolt from below, from within the Bangladesh army, was successful indeed. In the course of the morning, I saw Colonel Taher moving around a jeep near the Race Course area and, as he stopped briefly when seeing me, he informed me that there would be a public rally later that day. Before that, at dawn, Taher's brother Anwar had solemnly declared from the Dhaka radio, then the country's principal medium of communication with the population, that theirs was a soldiers'-people's uprising aimed at bringing social change. In the course of the day also, I saw groups of JSD supporters holding demonstrations in the city centre in support of the rising. Yet the rally which had been announced, and at which both Colonel Taher and Ziaur Rahman were to speak, never took place.

Nevertheless, in subsequent days, Dhaka was rife with rumours about soldiers' revolts in cantonments located in or near other cities. I received information, for instance that pamphlets of the Biplabi Sramik Sangstha had been distributed in the cantonment of Chittagong, and that rebelling soldiers had started on a march towards Dhaka from Jessore cantonment. Whereas these rumours were difficult to verify, it was evident that the state of Bangladesh had been paralysed, and that Taher's daring revolutionary attempt to this extent had been effective. The situation was only brought under control for the bourgeoisie after two weeks when Colonel Taher was arrested from the university area, and when a large drive was launched to arrest political activists belonging to the JSD. It is true—as saddened JSD supporters were later to insist—that the 1975 insurrection had a tragic outcome. The rising did not result in a transformation of the army, nor in emancipative change. Also the abortive revolt was followed by the gradual demise of the JSD. However, let us not forget for a moment when evaluating the past that the rising and its heroic leader were seen as a tremendous threat by Bangladesh's elite. Although Colonel Taher had been wounded and had lost a leg when leading a guerrilla force during the liberation war of 1971, his detention from late November till his hanging was accompanied by the most extraordinary security arrangements: the section of Dhaka central jail where he was detained was vacated so as to ensure that the state would not be brought down in another military rising under his lead.

The Soldiers' Uprising versus the Preceding Coups

I will now move on to record positive lessons to be drawn from the 1975 rising. There are basically three points that I wish to make. The first one relates to the difference between the soldiers' uprising and the two other army risings that preceded it in the same year. The series of risings was opened with the coup d'etat staged by the young 'Turks', a group of junior army officers, on August 15th against the rule of Sheikh Mujibur Rahman which had turned dictatorial. This uprising, precisely because it was directed against a government experienced as oppressed by broad sections of the population, was greeted with a sigh of relief: people in the streets of Dhaka, on August 15th, smiled. Yet the coup d'etat had more than one shady side: it was accompanied by the murder of a large part of Mujibur Rahman's family, and it had the backing of US imperialism, as many suspected from the start. On the morning of August 15th, I happened to be a silent witness to a confrontation, which took place at the Dhaka radio, between Colonel Taher and Mustaque Ahmed, leader of the pro-American wing of the Awami League. As Taher realised immediately, sections of Mujibur Rahman's own party were either directly involved in the coup or were ready to act in league with the young Turks. Historical research has since confirmed that it was a pro-American coup. The era of the rule of these young officers however was not to last very long. On November 2nd, Dhaka saw the beginning of another coup, when fighter planes were flown over the city in an apparent showdown between different factions of the army's leadership. I was able to collect data on this coup when later I happened to be detained in the very same cell of Dhaka central jail, where air force officers who had played a prominent role in the unfolding of the events of November 23rd, were held. These officers, all trained pilots, had entered jail as privileged personalities, being exempted from the harsh rules of submission that were imposed on other jail entrants. Subsequently, however, they were detained in a bullet-ridden cell, i.e. the very cell where four leading politicians of the Awami League had been killed in a bloody reaction against the November 3rd coup. According to the air-force officers, theirs had been a nationalist rising, contrary to the pro-imperialist coup of August 15th. Yet the Dhaka public had unanimously interpreted the November 3rd coup as restorationist, and its leader, Khaled Mosharaf was seen as pro-Awami League. In any case, just like its precursor, the November 3rd coup was staged 'from above' by ambitious army officers, who had risen to positions of military power in the wake of Bangladesh's 1971 liberation war. Neither the first nor the second coup of 1975 was inspired by ideals of social liberation, nor did the aspirations of common soldiers play an active part in shaping them. And here is where the third rising led by Taher was radically different in kind. The November 7th uprising was both in intent, i.e. as conceived by its principal leader, and in practice, as implemented by its participants, a soldiers' insurrection, an insurrection which, amongst others, targeted abolition of the unjust privileges held by the officers of Bangladesh's armed forces. Abu Taher had drawn his inspiration from a long historical tradition of soldiers' insurrections ranging from the first Indian war of independence, to the Bolshevik revolution of 1917, and the Velvet revolution which had brought down the fascist dictatorship in Portugal in 1974. A clear line of demarcation thus needs to be drawn between the third rising of 1975 and the two army risings that preceded it. Whereas the first two events were 'palace events', theatrical events played out between sections of Bangladesh's political and economic elite, the third event, the rising of November 7th, needs to be interpreted differently. It was a festival of the oppressed, in which Bangladesh's army soldiers spontaneously took part in huge numbers. No matter its drawbacks—November 7th was unique.

Taher's Vision of a People's Army

The second evaluative point concerns Taher's vision regarding the nature of the new state army to be built by independent Bangladesh. Taher had originally chosen a career as a military officer in the Pakistani army. He had received training at an American military academy. His exploits started in 1971 during Bangladesh's independence war. Like other Bengali officers in the Pakistani army, he rebelled to join the nationalist resistance. However whereas a number of officers could immediately cross lines, since they were stationed in (East) Bengal, Abu Taher could only join and participate after travelling a long way from an army garrison in Pakistan, via India's landmass towards the borders of occupied Bengal. Further contrary to other Bengali officers, Taher chose unequivocally to build a resistance army from within. In the far-northen region, he formed a guerrilla force recruited from among the local peasantry. One of the feats of this force was the famous Chilmari raid, in which the Pakistani garrison in the given town was attacked. It was very unfortunate that Taher got wounded, lost one leg and ended up in an Indian hospital. Thus, his dream of promoting a true liberation 'from within', i.e. primarily through efforts made independently from foreign patronage, could not be fulfilled.

Abu Taher, however, was garlanded as a hero of the liberation war and was then reintegrated as an officer in the state army of Bangladesh, formed soon after the country's formal independence in December 1971. It was then that the second chapter in Taher's saga started, for whereas most of the commanding officers of the new army held conenventional views regarding the place of the new army in Bangladesh's society, Taher's vision was distinct. The very first story which I recall having read about him was the one written by the American journalist Lawrence Lifschutz regarding his efforts to construct a production-oriented army. Being stationed as army commander in the Comilla cantonment, Taher instructd the soldiers to cultivate the soil, to grow pineapples so as to contribute to their own maintenance. Given the grinding poverty suffered by the majority of Bangladesh's population, the country in his view could not afford a colonial-type army without a productive role. The experiment in Comilla, however was not to last for long. Colonel Taher was dismissed from his army post. Although Mujibur Rahman in the folowing years continued calling him his 'golden son', Taher was sidelined and given a civilian task.

This in a nutshell was the path which Taher had followed since 1971 and which he continued to pursue via the soldiers' insurrection on November 7th. Surely preparations for the uprising had been discussed with other leaders of the opposition party the JSD, which Taher had secretly joined. Taher shared their broader vision in favour of a social revolution, a revolution to promote the emancipation of the society's oppressed. 'Our revolution', so it was proclaimed on the 7th 'is not a revolution aimed at replacing leaders but a revolution in the interests of the poor.' But central to the programmatic message was Taher's vision of a people's army. Although military preparations for the uprising were undertaken together with the 'Gana Bahini', the urban-centred guerrilla force formed as the armed wing of the JSD the agitation within the regular army was primarily carried out by secret units of the Biplobi Sramik Sangstha, the Council of Revolutionary Soldiers established under Taher's leadership. This Sangstha put forward a 12-point charter of demands, which notably included these demands: • that the differences between officers and soldiers be removed, • that officers be appointed on the basis of their merit, • that officers and soldiers be provided with the same rations and • that the system under which soldiers worked as personal servants of officers as batmen be abolished. Via the soldiers' insurrection of November 7th, Taher targeted, among other things, a thorough internal transformation of the state army of Bangladesh.

Military Strategy

The third point for evaluation—a point that is often overlooked—concerns the debate over military strategy within the Left of Bangladesh. In the immediate post-independence period of Bangladesh's history the influence of the Chinese model of revolution over various sections of the Bangladeshi Left was still large. I recall heated discussions between and with activists belonging to different underground Maoist party groups—debates over the strategy and tactics of revolutionary struggle which spilled into jails. Mao's key thesis is surely familiar. Since under China's semi-feudal conditions, the vast majority of the population lived in the countryside, where the presence of the reactionary state was weak the party needed to surround the cities from the countryside via a strategy of protracted people's war. The revolutionaries could best gather armed strength via a gradual process of accumulation, by building up a people's army via guerrilla actions in which selected units of the state's army were attacked and disbanded. Although Bangladesh's geographical and socio-economic conditions were rather different from those that had prevailed in pre-revolutionary China, in the years before Taher's soldiers' uprising, Mao's military strategy continued to be cherished by broad sections of the pro-Chinese Left in Bangladesh.

Against this background, Colonel Taher put forward a radically different thesis. In his view the Left needed to take notice of the fact that the Bangladesh state which had emerged in 1971 was a weak state, a state which lacked consolidated strength. In his view, Bangladesh's revolutionaries needed to forge the iron when it was hot. This they could do, Taher argued, by not primarily relying on the building of rural forces, though armed squads in the form of the *Gana Bahini* needed to be formed outside the urban centres as well. No, the principal area of confrontation in Bangladesh should be the country's capital where an armed uprising was entirely feasible. Not the strategy of protracted people's war would bring liberation for the country's oppressed but an insurrectionary military strategy. In meetings regularly held between us to reflect on the country's conditions, Taher could not openly express the fact that he prepared to stage an insurrection in the form of a soldiers' rebellion. Yet his conviction that only an insurrectionary strategy would do was stated without hesitation. There simply was no need for a prolonged and bloody revolutionary war since the road towards conquering state rule could be cut short.

I am recounting, re-summarising the historic controversy over revolutionary strategy in order to underline the significance of Taher's experiment. As stated, at a time when the dominant view was that the state army should be combated from without by forming guerrilla squads. Taher believed that instead the state army should be subverted from within, through agitation amongst the army's soldiers—agitating which should and which did lead to an explosion of soldiers' pent-up anger. Here, I may note in passing that a quarter century hence, even a section of Maoists have taken a more flexible view regarding the validity of protracted people's war. Thus, the party which has led the armed struggle for the abolition of the monarchy in Nepal, the CPN (Maoist), has admitted the possibility of a combined revolutionary strategy, one that includes both elements from the Chinese (people's war) and Russian (insurrectionary) experience. By staging a soldiers' insurrection, Colonel Abu Taher propagated the vision, and demonstrated the potential, of an insurrectionary strategy. And although with hindsight it is easy to criticise him for some of the tactics employed in implementing the vision described, it would be wrong to belittle the historical significance of Taher's revolutionary attempt.

Ireland and Bengal

I now wish to draw a comparison between the soldiers' rebellion led by Colonel Taher and another historical revolt which apparently failed, namely the Easter Rising in Ireland, staged in 1916. The comparison is for more than one reason valuable. To start, Ireland of course shares with Bangladesh a history of British colonial dominance. In fact, Britain's conquest over Ireland long preceded the British conquest over Bengal. Further, colonial rule in both cases deeply affected the social relations around, and the ownership of land. In Bengal, the zamindari system of feudal property relations, as we know was founded in consequence of the Permanent Settlement, declared in the late 18th century. In Ireland, the British ruler Oliver Cromwell reportedly dispossessed every Catholic landowner in the middle of the 17th century, when a reported eleven acres of land were confiscated and transferred to British ownership. Moreover, Britain's contempt of the peasantry in both cases resulted in terrible famines. The long series of famines which accompanied British rule over Bengal is all too familiar, a series which culminated in the horrible famine of 1943 claiming three million lives. Ireland lived in a most agonising crisis a century earlier, in 1846, when the cultivation of potato crop—the peasants' main staple food—failed for the second year in a row. Historical research on the 1943 Bengal famine has solidly established that it was mainly caused by Britain's war policies, policies such as the withdrawal of food resources, feeding the soldiers at the population's expense, and the financial drain of colonial India. In the case of Ireland, it was nature that played havoc with

Ireland's agriculture. Yet Britain was equally to blame, for in the face of a looming crisis the British rulers refused to act. They stuck to free market thinking, *laissez faire*, and thus 'caused Ireland to starve.'

I have summarised these shared characteristics between Bengal's and Ireland's history to underline how much these two countries have in common, even if we abstract from their parallel histories of militant people's resistance. There are differences, for instance, in the form of nationalism that were embraced by the Bengali and the Irish people, when struggling to overthrow British colonialism. Compared with Bengali nationalism, the profile of Irish nationalism seems strangely pre-modern. Whereas Bengali nationalism matured after Partition, during Pakistani rule, as an outgrowth of the movement for recognition of the Bengali language, Irish nationalism was not based on any indigenous language. For all sincere attempts to revive Gaelic in the later colonial period notwthstanding, the English language triumphed over Gaelic by the time Irish nationalism reached its maturity. Again, whereas the Bengali nationalism that succeeded in bringing people together in a common cause was explicitly secular in character championing religious tolerance, Irish nationalism in contrast was a religion-based nationalism. Here, Catholicism functioned as the common cultural denominator, unifying the Irish in opposition against the British rulers and their Protestant faith.

The above discourse on Irish history may sound like a diversion from today's topic, but it is very helpful towards understanding the significance of Irish history for an evaluation of the soldiers' uprising led by Colonel Abu Taher. Ireland has seen a failed armed uprising, and in this sense closely shares Bangladesh's historical experience. The experience is the abortive Easter Rising of 1916. The rising was no soldiers' insurrection, but like Bangladesh's rising, it was an armed attempt to capture state power, which in Ireland was then in the hands of the British. The bold uprising staged together by two armed resistance forces, including the leftwing Irish Citizens' Army led by James Connolly. On Easter morning, April

24, armed Irish fighters seized key public buildings in the centre of Dublin, Ireland's capital, and hoisted the Irish republican tricolour flag. The rising was crushed by the British, and its leaders were mercilessly executed. Yet the martyrdom of these heroes gave rise to a new wave of Irish nationalism, and helped pave the way for Ireland's war of independence. Forcing the British to relinquish its rule five years later (in 1921). What is specially noteworthy is the striking parallel between Taher's personal martyrdom, and the martyrdom of James Connolly, the Marxist thinker who was a key commander of the Easter Rising.Connolly was arrested while wounded with a leg shattered. As one of his biographers says, it was expected that he would not be killed, since one does not execute a wounded man. Yet Connolly, like Taher, had to die a martyr's death, because the oppressors saw him as too dangerous to let him live. Like Connolly, Colonel Taher was the leader of a 'pre-figurative' rising. Like him, Taher was a model of courage, a man who, in spite of his physical handicap, was too threatening to the oppressors' state to be allowed to live.

Taher's Legacy and Contemporary Politics

In conclusion, I would like to say a few words about Colonel Taher's contemporary significance, the significance of his ideas towards the struggles for social liberation in Bangladesh today. Speaking with hindsight, or with distance from the moment of the event it is perhaps not difficult to pinpoint some of the limitations of the 1975 soldiers' uprising. The soldiers, when moving through the streets of Dhaka in trucks were welcomed by the public, offered flowers as liberators from the threat of 'restoration'. They were seen as heroes preventing the return of oppressive bourgeois rule. Some attempts were apparently made to mobilise workers in support of the insurrectionists. Thus, Haidar Akbar Khan Rono mentions in his autobiography that industrial workers were brought to Dhaka from Tungi, then a key centre of power of Bangladesh's industrial working class, to demonstrate their support for the uprising. Yet the very weakest aspect of the 1975 uprising was the fact that the gap between different sections of the oppressed was not bridged. The peasants-in-arms, the soldiers, were not supported by a rising of the peasantry who at the time constituted the overwhelming majority of Bangladesh's population. Nor were industrial workers informed or alerted in time to join Taher's revolutionary attempt. Nevertheless the 1975 soldiers' insurrection was—to speak in line with Lenin's view of the Irish Easter rebellion—a great popular revolt. India had seen its first soldiers' uprising in 1857, an uprising which had completely shaken, destabilised British colonial rule. The uprising had a limited, but significant impact on the colonial army units stationed in Bengal and it surely contributd to the rise of nationalist temper amongst the colonised, both in British India at large and in the province of Bengal. Again, the anti-colonial resistance which reached its climax in the period immediately after the Second World War had its reverberatios in the colonial army. History books have recorded the naval revolt of 1946 which illustrated that Britain's colonial dominance over the subcontinent was untenable. Still, the idea of a soldiers' uprising when proposed by Colonel Tahe, was beyond the imagination of the Left in Bangladesh. Taher brought out the possibility of bouregeois rule from within the state apparatus. His primary lesson has thus to be upheld. We need a second version of the 1975 revolt in order to achieve the social liberation of Bangladesh's oppressed.

A second version, however, will inevitably need to take account of the revolution of Bangladesh's society since then. This primarily means that we need to take stock of the larger presence of wage-labourers in Dhaka city. Along with the huge influx of uprooted peasants from the countryside over the last thirty years, the number of industrial workers and informal sector workers has enormously grown in the capital. Today, as is well known, there are literally hundreds of thousands of readymade garment workers present in Dhaka and its surrounding areas who have an industrial exprience as labourers in readymade garment factories. In 2006, thirty years after the soldiers' revolt led by Abu Taher they staged their first insurrectionary attempt. Since then the sector has naturally been shaken by renewed upheavals, such as in June 2010, when militant struggles erupted in the Ashulia industrial area near Dhaka, and in Gazipur. Bangladesh's economy has undergone a dramatic transformation since the days of Colonel Taher's revolutionary attempt. So has the civil society, the sphere of society where a counter-hegemony of socialist ideas needs to be built. Yet as the country's workers and other sections of the oppressed resume their long struggle for liberation, they are bound to recall the one moment since independence, when bourgeois rule was thoroughly shaken—the days of the soldiers' insurrection led by the martyred Colonel Abu Taher.

Postscript

Colonel Abu Taher died a martyr's death on July 21, 1976, when he was executed by hanging in Dhaka Central Jail. The trial against him and other leading participants in the November 1975 rising was a farcical trial, and the execution was planned at the instruction of the country's military dictatorship led by Ziaur Rahman. The farcical nature of the trial has belatedly been exposed by Bangladesh's High Court which in March 2011, after a full re-hearing of the case, declared that the 1976 trial had been illegal and unconstitutional. The court therefore set the trial aside as fictitious, and ruled that Colonel Taher henceforth will be treated as a martyr and patriot. The unconstitutional nature of the trial followed from the fact that it had been instituted under martial law which itself had been contrary to the country's constitution. The High Court also noted numerous other irregularities, including the fact that the accused were not even told abut the charges they were to face, the fact they lacked access to lawyers and that they were barred from appealing against the then verdict. Undoubtedly, the High Court's 2011 verdict in the Taher case holds tremendously large significance. It not only is crucial in primary terms, i.e. in terms of justice to and rehabilitation of Colonel Taher and his associates. It also holds great positive significance for the cause of democracy, and for the emancipation of Bangladesh's oppressed.

REFERENCES

Ratan Lal Chakraborti. *Sipahijuddho O Bangladesh* (Bangla Academy, Dhaka, Bangladesh 1984).

Peter Custers, *Women in the Tebhaga Uprising. Rural Poor Women and Revolutionary Leadership* (1946-47), (Naya Prakash, Kolkata, India, 1987).

Abu Yusuf Khan, 'Deadline 7 November 1975' (*Bhorer Kagaz*, Dhaka, Bangladesh, November 7-12, 1994).

Haidar Akbar Khan Rono, *Satabdi Periye* (Tarafdar Prakashani, Dhaka, Bangladesh, 2005).

Riachard Kileen, *A Short History of Ireland* (Gill & Macmillan Ltd, Dublin, Ireland, 2005).

Lawrence Lifschultz, *Bangladesh: The Unfinished Revolution* (Zed Books, London, UK 1979).

Karl Marx, *Capital*, Vol. 1 (Progress Publishers, Moscow, USSR, 1977).

Liam de Paor (ed.), *Milestones in Irish History* (Mercier Press, Dublin, Ireland, 1998).

Altaf Parvez, *Ashamapta Muktijuddho*, Cornel Taher O Jasad Rajniti (Pathok Samabesh, Dhaka, Bangladesh, 1995).

Bernard Ransom, *Connolly's Marxsim* (Pluto Press, London, UK, 1980).

Suprakash Ray, '*1857 Khristabder Mahabidroha O Bangladesh*' (in *Bharater Krishak Bidroha O Ganatantrik Sangram*, Book World, Kolkata, 1990, pp. 342-469).

Idem, *Bidroi Bharat* (Book World, Kolkata, India, November, 1983).

(Autumn Number, 2011)

16

Democratic Deficit

Vaskar Nandy

Before the collapse of the actually existing socialist states (AES) and the transformation of Mao's China into Deng's China, informed observers from the whole political spectrum, with very few exceptions, were agreed that the state in those countries were by and large welfarist, providing social security of a fairly comprehensive character in spite of extensive under-development and maldevelopment. The welfare system did break down at short phases such as in the aftermath of the so-called collectivisation process in the Soviet Union and the Great Leap Forward in China. The basic features of this welfare state were universal access to the basics of education, housing and health care, and full employment. There were also quite significant forward movements towards greater equality. These countries were free of the untold miseries that visit workers in capitalist countries during the business cycle crises and depressions. These economies did not depend for their survival on military production (military Keynesianism).

Only diehard bourgeois publicists denied or ignored these features of the actually existing socialist states. Communists and other admirers of these states on the other hand would highlight these features as the defining markers of socialism. Those who subscribed to such views in spite of ample disclosures about terroristic states and the transformation of the Soviet Union into an expansionist superpower (rightly framed within the perspective of social imperialism) are either despairing now, or like Deng and his followers worldwide, such as the Communist Party of India (Marxist) are now the brazen servitors of the current gambling saloon capitalism, where the guns are not very far away.

As a welcome sign of change, *People's Democracy* (August 30, 2009), the weekly organ of the Communist Party of India (Marxist), carried an article, *Socialism and Welfarism*, by one of its ideologues which looks very briefly at the difference between a welfare state and genuine socialism. The author Prabhat Patnaik, who has expressed some unease about his party's line and practice, is mainly concerned with telling the flock that there is nothing wrong, indeed there is an imperative, to fight for a welfare state which the bourgeoisie is sometimes compelled to concede against its wishes or retract according to the ebb and flow of class struggle. This may or may not be a tangential commentary on the vigorous pursuit of neoliberal panaceas by his comrades in power in three Indian states. Be that as it may, but for our purposes here the most interesting point of the article was a denial that a welfare state in itself, even the best, is socialism. That immediately cuts the ground for the widespread defence of AES on the basis of Patnaik's opening paragraph raises a faint hope that those who still cling to the endorsement of everything since October 1917 to the 'collapse of socialism' will now begin a rethinking on socialism. 'Socialism consists', Patnaik writes, 'not just in building a humane society; it consists not just in the maintenance of full employment (or near full employment together with sufficient unemployment benefits); it consists not just in the creation of a welfare state, even one that takes care of its citizens "from the cradle to the grave", it consists not just in the enshrining of the egalitarian ideal. It is of course all this, but it is also something more. Its concern, as Engels had pointed out in *anti-Duhring*, is with *human freedom*,with the change in the role of the people from being *objects* of history to being its *subjects*, for which all the above conditions of society, namely full employment, welfare state measures, a reduction in social and economic inequalities, and the creation of a humane order, are necessary conditions; but they are not, seen in their aggregation, synonymous with the notion of freedom. And hence they do not exhaust the content of socialism.' Unfortunately for us, this author, with his own purposes in mind, does not go far into an analysis of the social and economic conditions for the development and condition of human freedom in the socialist process, the dictatorship of the proletariat. Presently, we intend to argue that this process, if it aspires to take society to communism, i.e. a classless, stateless society of associated labourers, must constitute itself on the basis of the widest democracy, a democracy that is well beyond the conceptions of the liberal bourgeoisie. That is the only basis on which the objects of history can become its subjects. Then why is there this use of the word 'dictatorship'? Dictatorship can be used in two senses, as a description of a form of government where a person, clique, party or the armed forces of the country run the government lawlessly, without the expressed consent of the governed. The other sense is more like law-governed, limited and extremely short-run, individual dictatorships brought in by the senate during emergencies, usually external aggression faced by the Roman republic. In the modern, most extreme example, the government may be liberal democratic with a regime constituted by universal franchise, but it is still a bourgeois dictatorship because the institutions of the state are founded upon and support the establishment, growth and stabilisation of the capitalist economic system and the power of the monopoly bourgeoisie to remain the ruling class. The US has never been a dictatorship (in the first sense) such as Somoza or Papa Doc, but capitalist, minority interests prevail over its constitutional system. It is thus a dictatorship of the bourgeoisie in the second usage. That is law-governed condition that does not directly violate the processes emanating from universal franchise or the general consent of the governed. Marx came to use the term in the second usage' as the form at last discovered' for the transition from the rule of capital to communism during the two month- long Paris Commune of 1871... The commune saga began by smashing the old bureaucracy, the standing army and other structures of the bourgeois state. One of the features of the dictatorship of the proletariat and the commune's plans for other cities and the countryside, much emphasised by Marx and Engels, was elections through universal franchise [1] to legislative- cum-executives at many levels of decentralised authority. These authorities were to be coordinated at many levels to converge nationally.

All delegates to higher coordinating bodies were to be mandated to express and support the resolutions of the delegating lower body. All elected posts (including those of judges, policemen, bureaucrats, etc) were subject to the right of recall. The previous armed forces were to be replaced by short-term service in the people's militias or army. No one, including all elected officials, could receive wages higher than those received by skilled workers.

This dictatorship of the proletariat is always established through a popular uprising by eliminating the ownership of the means of production, political power and the ideological state structures of the bourgeoisie. Lenin characterised the resultant society under the dictatorship of the proletariat as socialist. The usage has become more or less universal in spite of the protests of some very learned textual purists. Lenin sees socialism as a transition between the capitalist mode of production and a communist mode of production, classless and stateless.

Marx also spoke of this transition from the present capitalist mode of production to communism. He was very far from the reactionary concept floated by Soviet theoreticians of a socialist mode of production. 'Between capitalist and socialist society lies the period of the revolutionary transformation of the one into the other. There corresponds to this also a political transition period when the state can be nothing but the revolutionary dictatorship of the proletariat.' (Marx 1970) The task of this dictatorship is to effect the 'transition to the abolition of all classes and to a classless society'. It is also 'the declaration of the permanence of the revolution, the class dictatorship of the proletariat as the necessary transit point to the abolition of class distinctions generally, to the abolition of all relations of production on which they rest, to the abolition of all social relations that correspond to these relations of production, to the revolutionising of all the ideas that result from these social relations' (Marx 1977: 387).

Given the Marxian conception of the state as the instrument of rule by the exploiting classes this culmination point of the socialist process is necessarily a stateless society. This statelessness doesn't just arrive at the culmination but is one that begins at the very initiation of the process as a continuous withering away of the state. That means that the state of the dictatorship of the proletariat combines with itself growing elements of its negation, a non-state. From the 1930s onwards, Stalin questioned this concept of the withering away of the state even after his famous 1935 position that the Soviet Union had become classless.

Class is the crucial concept in the Marxist understanding. Lenin provided a well-rounded definition of this concept in an important article, 'A Great Beginning'.

Classes are large groups of people differing from each other by the place they occupy in a historically determined system of social production, by their relation (in most cases fixed and formulated in law) to the means of production, by their role in the social organisation of labour, and consequently, by the dimensions of the share of the social wealth of which they dispose and the mode of acquiring it. Classes are groups of people one of which can appropriate the labour of another owing to the different places they occupy in a definite system of social economy.

Clearly, in order to abolish classes completely, it is not enough to overthrow the exploiters, the landowners and capitalists, not enough to abolish their rights of ownership. (Lenin 1972; 421) Charles Bettelheim pointed out a long time ago that, according to Lenin here, the juridical ownership of the means of production is not a necessary condition for the determination of the place in the social organisation of labour and the consequent disposal and appropriation of social wealth.

Class is a crucial issue and relates to the distinction between the nationalisation of the means of production (which can be decreed) and socialisation which requires the most profound and extremely long-term social and political movement of the masses ('continuing the revolution under the dictatorship of the proletariat') over many generations.

What happens after the new state takes over the factories and the enterprises of the capitalists? The managers remain or are replaced by other managers and they work to a national plan prepared by some leading party body and various specialists who, along with the managers, were mostly socialised previously as functionaries of capital. The new situation and the newly established egalitarian ideology might or might not bring to their social consciousness new ideas, even revolutionary ones. But the chain of command still remains external to the worker as before when plant managers worked according to the order of the top management and owners. No only a different chain of command, from the Polit-Bureau-approved planning body to the plant managers and party leaders, presumably with a different outlook. At the beginninng, there is no way that such a centralised planning process can be avoided. With time, inputs and even challenges from below may be entertained in the service of modifying some feature of the plan. But in all AES countries this basic pattern of centralised plans that were to be implemented by factory managements remained till nearly the end. Yugoslavia after the break with the CPSU was an exception. But its enterprise of decentralisation recreated the value form in its own way.

Stalin summed up the system with its characteristic accuracy and brevity.

They (the means of production) are only allocated by the state to its enterprises. In the second place, when transferring means of production to any enterprise—the state—does not at all lose the ownership of them; on the contrary, it retains it fully. In the third place, the directors of enterprises who receive means of production from the Soviet state, far from being their owners, are deemed to be the agents of the state in the utilisation of the means of production in accordance with the plans established by the state. (Stalin 1972; 53)

It will be most instructive to read this Stalin paragraph by simply replacing the word 'state' with the word 'corporation.' As far as workers' ownership and control of the forces of production, nothing much seems to have changed. This hard reality cannot be wished away by idealistically reducing the identity of the workers to that of the self-professed party of the workers' vanguard which runs the state. It is now accepted all around that contrary to Stalin, the AES economic system as a whole, i.e. including exchanges within the state sector and not just in the exchanges between the state and the colletive sectors, was subject to the law of value. The Maoists were very clear about this. What does the value form rest on? According to Marx, the value form rests on 'different kinds of labour carried out independently of each other'. But where were the labourers in the quotation from Stalin? Now one knows that they were wage slaves, labourers performing different kinds of labour independently under the yoke of a ramified, all-powerful and extremely lawless bureaucracy.

Production of commodities and their echange through money transactions were not 'mere form', as Stalin thought, and just a device for calculation and settlement, for determining whether enterprises are runnng at a loss, for checking and controlling the enterprises. They were not the dialectician's famous nightmare, forms without content. These forms appeared and persisted because as their content was the fact that the labourers were not the possessors of the means of production, however loud the idealistic glamour about ownership by the working class. By their 'role in the social organisation of labour' (Lenin, above) the leaders of the party and the managers were the actual possessors and real owners of the means of production. That means that, as Chang (one of the 'gang of four') put it, there is a distinction between the formal and the actual settlement of the question of ownership. Only the workers' assertion, participation and control over the processes of production and, hence, distribution, can gradually break down the division of labour between managers and labourers, a social relation of production that rests squarely on the ownership question.

This role in the social organisation of labour marks the leaders of the party and the managers employed by them as a class in itself that could aspire through totalitarian state terror and the imposition on the workers an ideology that mimics living Marxism to become a class for itself. That is precisely what happened in the AES countries.

The kind of time-scale Mao had in mind for the journey to communism can be gauged from his talking about the seizure of power as the first step in a ten thousand li[2] march. He made another vey significant statement on this issue near the end of his life in 1974, more than twenty years after the seizure of power in China.

"In a word, China is a socialist country. Before liberation she was much the same as a capitalist country. Even now she practises an eight-grade wage system, distribution according to work and exchange through money and in all this differs very little from the old society." (Quoted in Cang Chun Chiao 1975:5)

The protracted nature of the process can be gauged by its complexity. Chang Chun Chiao (who had led the working class of Shanghai to start building a commune on the pattern of Paris during the height of the Cultural Revolution but was dissuaded by Mao himself) urged communists to 'see more clearly that on the problem of the system of ownership, as on all other problems, one should pay attention not only to its form, but also to its actual content. It is perfectly correct for people to attach importance to the decisive rule of the system of ownership in the relations of production. But it is incorrect to attach no importance to whether the issue of the system of ownership has been resolved in form or reality. ....The correctness or incorrectness of the ideological and political line, and the control of leadership in the hands of one class or another, decides which class owns a factory.' (Quoted in Chang Chun Chiao 1975:9) The passage from Stalin shows quite clearly which class was leading production.

This question of leadership is crucial and it raises the

question of the role of the party under the dictatorship of the proletariat. In all AES countries, 'Marxist-Leninist' parties, proclaiming themselves to be the vanguard of the proletariat, instituted single party rule. They controlled the standing armies, the bureaucracies and, if it existed, the judiciary. The trade unions ceased to be organs for the self-organisation and education for workers and became appendages of the party. Their task was to cheer onerous work norms and higher production, while subjecting all dissent from workers to ridicule or punishment. Only those ideas that received the approval of the party could be seen in the media; all contrary ideas were silenced and the people who held them were punished severely. Instead of argument, there was censorship. In the Soviet Union, the party proclaimed itelf to be monolithic and soon devoured all minority opinion within it and without. In China, the party was viewed more dialectically, as one that contained two-line struggles. Some of those struggles were tolerated but many important ones were not. Extreme secrecy shrouded internal debate and whatever leaked out was only the rant of the victorious.

The vanguard parties in Russia, Yugoslavia, Albania and China earned the prestige of leading the masses to victory against reactionaries through insurrection and war. They presided over the total expropriation of the erstwhile ruling classes, including not just their property but also their linkages to the ideological state structures and the media. The bourgeoisie's links to the armed forces vanished with the liquidation of those forces. But their linkages to those sections of the bureaucracy that had to be retained to help in the running of the vast, newly acquired state properties, although weakened, could not be obliterated. But sooner than later, the system described by Stalin above was imposed upon the labouring masses. Such parties were then well on their way to becoming the vanguard of the new bourgeoisie. The Gorbachevs and the Yeltsins, all top leaders of the CPSU, pretend no longer to any communist identity, having abandoned their country to criminals, gangsters and the suave persuaders of the shock therapy. Treading the neoliberal path by other means, Deng's cohorts continue to identify themselves as the vanguard of the proletariat.

This self-identification as a vanguard has no source of validation other than its own power in the AES countries. With this identification and in the pretended interest of suppressing the bourgeoisie this party has made a mockery of universal franchise. Appointment or removal of its candidates to state office, high or low, follows Byzantine processes within its own fold, without even a nod towards the workers whose highest representatives they are supposed to be.

The example of the mass participatory democracy of the commune is eschewed on the ground that the bourgeoisie, obviously the old ones who have lost property, the powerful media and the backing of the bureaucracy and the armed forces will apparently make a return if multi-party elections with a universal franchise are institutionalised. Of course such an outcome is not entirely unthinkable, especially if the workers feel oppressed by the workings of the new, actual owners of the means of production and distribution. But what does a return mean? Will the old bourgeoisie resume its ownership of the means of production and all the power that such ownership bestows? Hardly likely. A working class that rose in insurrection or people's war precisely to divest the bourgeoisie of such ownership or power would not tolerate such an outcome. But suppose it does so. What does that prove? It proves that the rule by the vanguard was worse than what their memories tell them of the old regime. The party will be on its way to truly play the vanguard role if it signposts such an outcome as the proof of its gross mistakes and changes its policies towards being the servants of the masses and not their masters. A communist party that has lost the workers' mandate must not only rectify its mistakes but must in adversity be prepared to go underground, as before the revolution, to regain that mandate.

The question of the armed forces is very important. The AES countries institutionalised standing armies. These have always been the instruments of the last resort in the maintenance or the capture of power, as in the case of the Beijing garrison arresting the majority of the Polit Bureau clearing the way for the seizure of power by the neoliberals (with Confucian characteristics) led by Deng. To be sure, the dictatiorship of the proletariat does need armed forces to quell bourgeois rebellion of the Kolchak and Denikin type and external aggression. But if the workers are to have real power under the dictatorship of the proletariat, these armed forces must take the character of an armed people, as envisaged by the commune. Only then can the workers express their will, right or wrong, according to their experience. Mistakes are always possible but the workers' right to make mistakes is fundamentally linked to their self-education and the gradual rise to become the ruling class.

No one-party rule no unelected bureaucrats no standing army, and multi-party elections under universal franchise and the right of recall should be on the musts of every communist party. Only then can workers begin to express thmselves and begin the long journey to remould themselves and their circumstances in a process of doing and learning. In a simultaneous process the communist party will also remould itself to arrive asymptotically to a real, not self-proclaimed, integration with the movement of the working class. Just like the state, the party will also begin to wither away.

That is the freedom road, the road to being the subjects of history and not its objects.

NOTES

1. That universalism did not extend to the heroic women of Paris who were at the forefront of the armed struggle against Versaills.
2. The *li* is a traditional Chinese unit of distance, which has varied considerably over time but now has a standardised length of 500 metres or half kilometre. (c.1640 feet)

REFERENCES

Chang Chun Chiao, 1975. *On Exercising All-Round Dictatorship Over the Bourgeoisie*, Peking, Foreign Language Press.

Lenin, V.I., 1972. 'A Great Beginning', *Collected Works*, Vol. 29. Moscow,

Progress Publishers, 409-34.

Marx, Karl, 1970. 'Critique of the Gotha Programme' in Marx/Engels *Selected Works,* Vol. 3. Moscow, Progress Publishers, 13-30.

Marx, Karl, 1977. *Collected Works,* Vol. 10. Moscow, Progress Publishers.

Stalin, J.V., 1972. *Economic Problems of Socialism in the USSR,* Peking, Foreign Language Press.

(September 27 – October 3, Source: For a New Democracy, October 2009-March 2010)

List of Contributors

Timir Basu, a postgraduate in geology, was a student leader and a trade-union activist, besides being a freelance writer. He has served as the editor of *Frontier* ever since the death of Samar Sen, its founder editor, in 1987.

Anirban Biswas taught economics for three decades at Krishna Chandra College, Birbhum, West Bengal and has written two books, *Cowrie Currency of India* and *Money and Markets from Pre-colonial to Colonial India*. He is currently the assistant editor of *Frontier*.

Late *Hiren Mukherjee*, a distinguished student of history, was a famous parliamentarian belonging to the CPI, and was known for his graceful style of writing and brilliant oratory. He authored several books including *India's Struggle for Freedom, The Gentle Colossus*, and *Gandhiji - A Study*.

Partha Chatterjee, a renowned social scientist, has long been associated with the Centre for Studies in Social Sciences, Kolkata. For several years, he has been a professor of social Anthropology in Columbia University. He is the author of many books, including *Bengal: the Land Question, A Princely Impostor? - The Kumar of Bhawal and Secret History of Indian Nationalism, Nation and Its Fragments*, etc. He has written for *Frontier* for more than three decades.

Dipanjan Ray Chaudhuri, a distinguished student and teacher of physics, has been associated with people's movements for a long time and contributed many articles to *Frontier* and other radical journals.

Saral Sarkar, a former lecturer of German at the Goethe Institute, Hyderabad, is the author of several books including *Green-Alternative Politics in West Germany, Eco-Socialism or Eco-Capitalism?, The Crisis of Capitalism* etc.

Subhas Ghatade is a social activist and freelance journalist who has been writing continuously on various problems of Indian society.

T.Vijayendra is a social activist and environmentalist, who is a regular contributor to *Frontier*.

Gayatri Chakravorty Spivak is asscoiated with the University of Columbia, USA. She is a noted historian associated with the Subaltern Group.

Jan Myrdal, a Swedish intellectual and son of Nobel Laureate Gunner Myrdal, is a tireless fighter for people's rights and civil liberties. His books include *Confessions of a Disloyal European, India Waits, Red Star Over India*, etc.

Aloke Mukherjee, an engineering graduate, has been associated for nearly five decades with left political movements as a whole-time political activist and has written extensively on many subjects on politics and history.

Paresh Chattopadhyay is a well-known Marxologist who taught at the Indian Institute of Management, Kolkata, University of Paris and University of Quebec, Montreal. He contributed numerous articles to various journals like *Frontier, Econmic and Political Weekly* and *Monthly Review*.

Ranjit Sau, a noted economist, taught for many years at the Indian Institute of Management, Kolkata, University of Calcutta and a number of universities in the USA. He also authored several books including *Indian Economic Growth: Constraints and Prospects, Unequal Exchange: Imperialism and Development, Underdeveloped Capitalism and the General Law of Value, India's Economic Development: Aspects of Class Relations, etc.* and numerous articles on economics and various other subjects. He also contributed to *Frontier* and *Economic and Political Weekly* for about three decades.

Santosh Rana, a distingushed student of physics and a leader of the historic Gopiballavpur peasant uprising in Medinipur in West Bengal, 1969-70, is a prolific writer and translator, who has written extensively on the question of

Dalits and other identities in India as well as on the problems of Marxism, mainly in Bengali. His two collections of essays are *Samaj, Sreni O Rajniti* (Society, Class and Politics) and *Ganatantra O Bampantha* (Democracy and Leftism).

The late *Peter Custers* was a Dutch social activist and research worker who wrote intensively on the historic Tebhaga Movement of Eastern India particularly on women's participation in it. He was also an expert on the people's movements in Bangladesh.

Vaskar Nandy, educated at University College of London and Columbia University, has been associated with people's movements for more than five decades and written numerous illuminating articles on various subjects relating to such movements, particularly on those in Assam and North Bengal. He has also written several articles on the nationality question, problems of socialism, etc.